If there's one thing I've learned …

HOW TO SEIZE YOUR
ONCE-IN-A-LIFETIME CHANCE
TO GET IT RIGHT

JAMES GREEN

Sound View Publishing, Inc.
Shoreham, New York

Sound View Publishing, Inc.
Post Office Box 696
Shoreham, NY 11786-0696
www.SoundViewPublishing.com
1-888-529-3496

ISBN 0-9761058-4-5
Library of Congress Control Number: 2004112899

Printed in the United States of America
Book design by Sara Patton
Back cover writing by Write to Your Market

Educational institutions, business organizations, and book clubs:
Quantity discounts are available on bulk purchases of this book for reselling, educational purposes, subscription incentives, gifts, or fundraising. For more information, contact Sound View Publishing, Inc. (call 1-888-529-3496 or visit www.SoundViewPublishing.com).

If interested in having James Green speak or give a seminar to your company, association, school, or organization, please visit www.SoundViewPublishing.com or call 1-888-529-3496.

To my son Kevin.

In you I see everything.

Warning/Disclaimer

Contents

IN A WHISPER 1

DREAMS AND AWAKENINGS 5

Nantucket and a fleeting glimpse 7

A body of evidence 10

Risk and reward 11

The pretty lady 13

The dancer 16

If you're going to San Francisco 18

No Andy Warhol 20

Succinctly speaking 21

Baking in a boxcar 21

An American in Florence 25

Decisive moments 28

Christmas morning 30

Making her own way 32

A whisper and the Dark Continent 35

THE ONE WHO GOT AWAY 39

Wearing a white dress 41

<u>Underlined in black</u> 43

Good girl, bad girl 45

Sitting on my hands 47

The faceless man 49

Did Pete call? 52

Hoping he'd turn around 55

There's something about Stephanie 57

CAREERS 63

Ten feet tall and bulletproof 65

Going to the chapel 68

Who I am 70

Your own totem pole 72

Eyes open 74

Nine years and eleven months 76

The natural choice 79

Political science 81

Windows that open and close 82

People knowledge 83

The echo effect 86

The gift 87

The river visual 90

OUR FRIENDS AND FAMILY 93

The only thing 95

Sinners and saints 96

Ramifications 98

How cavalier 100

Emotional ice cube 102

Iron men 104

A note for my mother 106

Magic hour 107

I never saw him again 108

A strong son 109

My mentor 111

Courage 112

Carry that weight 113

I can't remember 114

Her life 116

Friend to a friend 117

For my grandmother 118

Chinks in the armor 120

Gone fishing 121

RELATIONSHIPS, LOVE, AND MARRIAGE 123

I wouldn't presume 125

A borrowed man 125

Cyber sex and the Sirens' song 129

Love is a girl's best friend 132

She liked me 135

Barefoot in Toronto 137

MONEY AND FINANCE 141

My money 143

Guitars and amps and crap 143

Out of pocket 144

Know money, or no money 146

Crazy money 148

Cash or charge? 149

Bet your bottom dollar 150

Today 152

The richest man in the graveyard 153

LOOKING BACK: WHISPERS OF HIGH SCHOOL, COLLEGE, AND THE ARMED SERVICES 157

Purely by accident 159

Nobody gets into Stanford 162

The role of the airhead 164

Three letters 166

I *am* smart 168

Cute and funny 170

Trust 171

Now she knows 173

Turn the other cheek? 176

Fiefdoms 178

Postscript 179

KINDNESS 183

Thinking of you 185

A kid like Bobby 185

Judgment 188

The sign of the cross 191

Passing by 193

A man in Manhattan 197

PERSPECTIVE 201

The edge 203

Fate wears a backpack 203

On an October afternoon 209

TIME **213**

As you walk by (The unexpected) 215

A jumbo bag of M&M's 218

Sail away 220

That sex thing 222

Surely, she doesn't mean it 222

The 80/20 rule (My perfect life) 223

The starter's pistol 225

The old guy 226

When they were 64 227

Hi Buddy 228

Blocking for me 229

They say life is long 230

I remember 232

INTERVIEW QUESTIONS **235**

INDEX **241**

Acknowledgments

Dave Dunlap, thank you for your friendship, and that one perfect idea that started it all.

Graham Van Dixhorn of Write to Your Market, your patience and professionalism were greatly appreciated.

Marilyn Ross, your guidance was instrumental in helping me complete this book.

Sara Patton, you helped make the uncomfortable comfortable.

Dunn+Associates, thank you for delivering an inspired cover design.

Very special thanks to my parents, friends, and extended family for tolerating my sometimes intolerable behavior while I was pursuing this project.

To my wife Peggy, thank you for your understanding and forgiveness during the time spent soliciting and conducting interviews, the endless string of phone calls and conferences, and all of those days and nights spent writing and rewriting this manuscript.

All of my proofreaders deserve my deepest thanks. Without their guidance, there would be nothing on these pages. Thank you Joann Graziano, David Dunlap, Diane Casey, Patricia Green, Linda Cummings, Teresa McDonald, Alfred and Joy Abbato, Peggy Green, Pat DiCarlo, Karen Furgal, Robert Dunlap, Russ Hampel, Joan Worontzoff, Jeffrey Carter, and Lori Dunlap.

*To know the road ahead,
ask those coming back.*

Chinese proverb

Preface

To better understand the message of this book, we can begin by discussing all of the things that it is not. It is not a "brush your teeth and do your homework" rehash of what your mother always told you to do. It is not a lecture about the seven deadly sins, the Boy Scout code of conduct, traffic laws, or any other set of rules by which we live our lives. It is about the choices we make every day. It is about the future.

Unlike using psychics or horoscopes in an attempt to know what is ahead, there is no magic in this book. No tables that rise, no knocking from behind the wall. In these pages, our future peeks out at us from behind the stories and experiences of others.

All of the stories in this book have been drawn from the interviews I have conducted. In all cases, I have changed the names of those with whom I spoke in order to protect their privacy. Several people also requested that their occupations be changed.

In order to solicit interviews, I took out ads in newspapers and community circulars. I spoke to various clubs and organizations. After that, referrals accounted for the majority of my interviews. (A list of my interview questions has been included at the end of the book.)

My stories and comments are scattered throughout this book. Any story that is *not* labeled with a name, age, and occupation belongs to me. If I interject my comments in another person's story, my thoughts appear italicized.

After countless conversations covering scores of topics, what became clear to me is that regardless of who you are or what you want, life offers a road map. There are many wonderful things for us to do, but perhaps more importantly, an even greater number of things *not* to do. The stories shared in this book represent what has worked in the lives of others and what has not. They serve as examples *and* warnings.

Just as different people understand different languages, not every story will speak to every reader. The idea is to listen to the various voices and make your own decisions. When one of them speaks to you, you'll know it.

You cannot teach a person anything;
you can only help him find it within himself.

Galileo Galilei (1564–1642)
Italian astronomer, physicist, philosopher

In a whisper

We all have the opportunity to choose our future. It is always there, rolled out in front of us, ready for us to step into it, step around it, or ignore it and let it slip by. It is unmarked and waiting for us, arms folded. Not impatiently, but calmly, confident in its inevitability.

We can live in no other moment but the present, so how do we control our future? How do we choose our path and find our way through the trees?

If we had to rely solely on ourselves, we could use our past experiences as the lamp that lights our feet. We could look back upon our lives to learn the lessons, and then apply them forward. Although that is certainly a successful approach, thankfully there are even better ways to know what's ahead.

The only real way to get some sense of our future is to listen to the stories of those who have wandered farther down the path ahead of us. Those who have done and seen what we have not yet done and seen. What lessons have *they* learned? What experiences have they had that we would like to either emulate or avoid? If we take the lessons that others have learned and apply them forward in *our* lives, we truly have a window on our future.

Despite the gains we make when we *do* ask about what's ahead, most of the best questions go unasked. The good advice shouted back from over the shoulders of those in front of us often goes unheeded. Why is this so? Is it because we do not trust the source? Is it because we tend to ignore advice on everything but the most superficial of subjects?

Perhaps the secret is not in the questions we ask. If we know what the important questions are, maybe we only need to listen for the answers. Every day, there are answers being shouted back from those ahead of us. Based upon those answers, the most important questions seem to be: What are the things that I need to do in this life? What will I regret? What and who will I cherish? When all is said and done, what will matter the most to me?

At key moments along the path when life asks us to choose, our future rarely shouts; it whispers. "*This* will matter. *This* is important." You can call that whisper anything you like—fate, providence, chance, luck, God, destiny—but it's really something more connected than that. The whisper tells us the things we'll one day wish we knew now, the things we'll someday wish we had understood earlier.

My life has greatly benefited from listening to that whisper. One of the earliest and most important times I heard it was when I was around 21 years old. It was just a simple newspaper article but it changed everything for me.

The story was about an amazing 60-year-old man whose life was forever changed when, at the age of 15, he heard his adult relatives complaining about all of their regrets. Hearing that, the young man wrote out a list of everything he ever wanted to see, do, or achieve. The rest of his life was guided by that list, his life list.

The life list *I* created soon after reading that article was the blueprint for everything that followed. Although I did not fully understand it at the time, reading that story put me on a new path. It whispered to me, and in its strangely familiar voice I heard the message that would help guide the rest of my life.

From that moment to this, as I type these words, I have measured everything I have ever done as if I were old and gray, looking back on it from far in the future. It has been this obsession, the obsession with directing my future and avoiding a life of regret, which has driven me to write this book. It occurred to me that if my life was changed by a simple story, then perhaps other lives could be changed through a collection of stories.

The stories in this book are yours. They are the stories of *your future,* just told by others here in the present. As you read this book, think of yourself as Ebenezer Scrooge from Charles Dickens's *A Christmas Carol.* These stories represent the shadows of what could be, what might be. Like Ebenezer, in the end, it is up to you to decide how the story of your life will be written.

I would never presume to tell you how you should live your life. All I ask is that you listen to these voices. Hearing them is not enough; you have to listen. Sometimes the volume of these voices is as deafening as a scream, but their message is always given in a whisper.

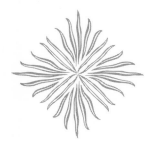

Dreams and Awakenings

*Twenty years from now you will be more
disappointed by the things that you didn't
do than by the ones you did do. So throw
off the bow lines. Sail away from the safe
harbor. Catch the trade winds in your sails.
Explore. Dream. Discover.*

Mark Twain (1835–1910)
American writer, humorist, and lecturer

Nantucket and a fleeting glimpse

One of my earliest flying jobs was working for a commuter airline. We flew 19-seat turbo prop airplanes to towns and cities all over the northeastern United States and eastern Canada. The nature of the flying often required us to spend the night in those places. Most of those overnights were dull and routine but not all of them. There were a few wonderful places along the way.

One of my favorite overnights was on Nantucket. For those of you who are unfamiliar, Nantucket is a beautiful island just 15 miles south of Cape Cod, Massachusetts. It's a wonderful place with lots of New England charm and history.

Arriving there as a copilot was the first time I had been back to Nantucket since I was about 13 years old. My memories of the island were the sort of things a 13-year-old might remember: the boats, the grassy dunes near the shore, the cobblestone streets. Looking through the eyes of a 28-year-old, I saw for the first time what an incredible place it was for young people.

The center of town teemed with high school and college kids of every description. Some were visitors like me, but most were working: waiting tables, selling ice cream, things like that. Many wore restaurant "staff" shirts and hustled down the sidewalks on their way to or from work. There were shouts and greetings from across the street as various kids recognized one another. Whether it was on foot or by car, bicycle or skateboard, those kids moved with the spirit and vibrancy of youth.

Like most of the kids who summered in those resort towns, they probably lived in crowded seasonal rentals that were as fun and exciting as they were chaotic. I'm sure that when they were at work, they worked, but otherwise there were parties to attend, townies to meet, beach bonfires to build, and hearts to break. Despite all of those wonderful distractions, I'll bet that just being off on their own was enough. That first taste of independence probably made it all worthwhile.

After looking around, I realized that, if I'd had more courage at their age, I would have worked there too. When I was younger, I knew people who spent their summers living and working in those New England resort towns. They were kids I went to school with, kids whose names I knew. I always wanted to join them, but just the thought of doing something that independent and different so far from home scared me to death. Back then, I listened to my fears. Back then, I stayed home.

Over the next four and a half years, my job as a copilot brought me back to Nantucket almost every month. Part of my overnight ritual was to wander out from the old inn where we stayed and get a bite to eat in one of the quaint restaurants near the center of town. Afterwards, I wouldn't walk back to my room right away but would linger out on those cobblestone streets for a while, watching everyone walk by. I'd stand there just looking, just listening.

Seeing those kids laugh and flirt with one another made me think about how my life might have been if I had had less fear when I was younger. Whatever it was that I saw in their faces, I was old enough to recognize that it was out of my reach, but still young enough to think, if I just twisted around fast enough, I could still snatch it up from somewhere in the dust behind me.

Rediscovering Nantucket was wonderful, but it was also a bit sad.

Seeing that beautiful place again made me realize I had let something special slip past me. It wasn't as if the place itself had disappeared; the island would always be there. It was the *moment* that was gone. It was a life and a moment in time I wanted to choose and could have easily chosen, but did not. Despite all of its beauty and appeal, Nantucket will always serve as a reminder that there was once something wonderful waiting for me behind one of life's doors but I was too afraid to turn the knob.

The memory of those nights on the streets of Nantucket made me wonder if there were others who had similar experiences or regrets. The interviews I conducted showed me that although there were people who awoke in time from their fears and limiting beliefs, there were many who did not. There were those who awoke too late, and those who never awoke at all.

I asked those I interviewed if their awakenings had changed their lives. Did they realize too late the importance of something? Did they come to gain insights about themselves that they wish they had learned earlier? What, if anything, *did* they learn? Did they catch what they ran after, or were they still running? Did they even remember to run?

In the years since my awakening on those cobblestone streets, I visited as many New England resort towns as I could. Places like Nantucket, Martha's Vineyard, Hyannis, Block Island, and Newport became some of my favorite haunts. My reasons for going don't really matter. What matters is that I went. What matters is that never again did I want to feel that feeling—the way I felt the day I realized I had let something wonderful slip forever behind me.

Every year, my family spends a week in Newport, Rhode Island. Every year, we see a fresh batch of high school and college kids out on their own, working, living, and just taking the time to be young. As if by some prearrangement, they all wear the same thing: boat shoes, baggy shorts, and college sweatshirts. Also, as if prearranged, they all seem to be having the time of their lives. I envy those kids.

Go confidently in the direction of your dreams.
Live the life you have imagined.

Henry David Thoreau (1817–1862)
American author and philosopher

 # A body of evidence
(Lou, retiree, 64)

When I was younger, I thought people who went to the gym were narcissists. They always struck me as being self-indulgent, egotistical people. I prided myself on the fact that I was too busy working and raising my family to be so self-involved or so leisurely.

I used to look at all of those fitness fanatics and wonder, *Why aren't they out there working? Why aren't they out there doing what they have to do rather than doing all of these selfish things?* It took me 35 years to figure it out, but now I know why.

Now at my age, I regret not taking care of myself. To say I'm out of shape is putting it mildly. I'm about a hundred pounds overweight, and it's put a tremendous strain on my body. My hip is pretty bad and a lot of my joints are arthritic. Just getting out of a chair is now a major undertaking.

My doctor has put me on a diet and exercise program, but I'm digging myself out of a pretty deep hole. I feel pretty weak most of the time and I don't seem to have the strength to do the exercises my doctor prescribed. *That's* a big part of the problem. I've been doing the wrong things for so long, trying to do the right things now *feels* wrong.

It's not too late for me to change, but when I wake up in the morning it sure feels like it. I usually lie there for a few minutes just trying to work up the energy to get out of bed. It's going to take a considerable amount of hard work and rehabilitation for me to recover from this, assuming I *can* recover. Bad habits can be hard things to undo.

A lot of people I knew years ago had the discipline and foresight to take better care of their bodies. Wherever they are today, I'm sure they don't have the problems I have now. I took my health for granted, and I just hope it isn't too late.

> *Men of ill judgment oft ignore the good that lies*
> *within their hands, till they have lost it.*

Sophocles (496–406 B.C.)
Greek playwright, poet, and politician

 ## Risk and reward
(Craig, airline pilot, 34)

In 1988, back when almost no one was making or buying home computers, I came up with the idea to build and sell my own PC's. After hearing me talk about it, my friend Vic was anxious to get involved. We decided to be partners.

We were both 20 years old and still juniors in college. We had a lot of enthusiasm but we didn't know how to approach the idea. At first, we didn't let our age or our present situation get in the way of our plans. We talked constantly about how and where we would start our business. It was an exciting time.

Even though I was very interested in the idea, I also had dreams of becoming a pilot. Would it make sense for me to put that much effort into something else? A computer business would be very time-consuming and risky too. Vic and I were both full-time students and we worried about burning the candle at both ends. At the time, we did not let these concerns get in our way.

Vic said that we could use his mother's house to store our parts and to build the computers. I had been working with computers for years so I was confident in my ability to put together anything that a customer would want. All of the components were readily available and very affordable too.

We didn't really have a marketing plan yet, but we knew enough people on campus to get a good "word of mouth" campaign going. If need be, we could always have advertised in the school paper or even the smaller local papers. It really was the perfect place to start a business like that.

Of the three biggest problems we faced—work space, customer support, and start-up capital—the money was the only one we didn't really work on. We knew that there'd have to be some initial outlay of cash, but we did not talk about that aspect of the plan seriously. I had some money, but I was going to use it for the rest of my flight training. The computer business seemed risky, whereas the airline business seemed completely safe. Because I didn't want to risk my own money, *and* because we didn't see any other way to raise capital, everything just stopped. This perceived snag caused my enthusiasm to dry up.

Looking back, we never even *tried* to raise money for the business. There were so many things we could have done, so many places we could have looked, and so many people we could have asked. We did nothing.

At the time, Vic was just spinning his wheels, looking for any opportunity that might come his way. If I would have followed through, he *definitely* would have done it. It was my lack of determination that stopped the project. I'm the one who pulled the plug on the whole thing.

Now I'm an airline pilot. Because of September 11 and the changes in the economy that followed, my career as a pilot has turned out to be far riskier than any computer business I could have started. It's been really tough. I got let go from my job at one of the major airlines, but luckily, I managed to get hired at one of the new start-up airlines. My fingers are crossed that my new job will last.

Now that things are bad in my profession, my wife and I talk about that missed opportunity a lot. It's at times like these I wish I had a business on the side. With a house, a wife, and a daughter to take care of, it seems harder to get something else going. Right now, Vic is a successful attorney who runs a real estate business on the side. He's a real hard-charging guy.

Michael Dell founded Dell Computers while he was a freshman in college. He started putting computers together and selling them when he was still in *high school*. Look at him now.

I really regret not taking a shot at my own business. Maybe we would have crashed and burned, but maybe not. Hey, we'll never know.

The gods cannot help those who do not seize opportunities.

Chinese proverb

The pretty lady
(Lori, retired elementary school teacher, 60)

I've been overweight my entire life. My family never knew how to handle my weight problem or what to say to me. I wasn't exactly the best-looking kid on the block either, and maybe they didn't know how to deal with that.

What my grandmother said about me the day I was born says it all. According to my mother, the first thing she said when she saw me was, "Oh my, she's ugly." That's the self-image I've carried my entire life.

When you're heavy or considered unattractive, you're invisible. To give you an example of this sort of thing, many years ago, I was stuck at the side of the road in a bad snowstorm. I stood outside my car and waited for help for a long time, but no one stopped. After a while, my good friend Judy drove by and saw me standing there. She stopped to see what was wrong.

She saw I was stuck and realized she wouldn't be able to help push my car out. Knowing how the world is, I had an idea. Judy was really cute, thin too. I said to her, "Judy, just go and stand out there where everyone can see you." In about five minutes, we had more people stop to help than we knew what to do with. *That's* the type of invisibility I'm talking about.

My life went on like that until just a few years ago. Things changed for me on this one summer day that I picked my mother up from the hospital. The huge parking lot was almost completely full and the only space I was able to get was way out at the edge. It was a blazing hot day and I wasn't looking forward to pushing her wheelchair that far.

They released my mom from the hospital and we headed off across the parking lot. The incredible heat and my extra weight made my car seem a million miles away. Suddenly a man I had never met before said, "Excuse me. Do you need help pushing that wheelchair?" I was so startled that I jumped a bit. I didn't know what to do. As politely as I could, I refused his offer. He just smiled and walked away.

As I pushed my mother towards the car, I thought about what had just happened. Why did that man's offer startle me? Why was I so surprised? Before I got to the car, I found myself starting to cry.

His small act of kindness, his offer to help me, had really moved me. I was happy, but at the same time I was very embarrassed. What had my life become that I would be so affected by such a simple gesture? What strange little world did I live in to be shocked by the kindness of a stranger? The truth is, I was crying because for the first time in a long time, I wasn't invisible. Someone had finally seen me.

That small moment was a turning point in my life. The feelings of unworthiness that I carried were absolutely shameful. I was so embarrassed by my lack of self-worth that I got angry. I got angry at myself for allowing everyone else's opinions to dictate how I felt about myself. After that, I decided that there would be no more self-loathing for me. That was it.

Have you ever seen that famous ink drawing of the beautiful young Victorian-era woman? It's one of those weird drawings that if you look at it long enough, it changes. Instead of seeing the beautiful young woman, you'll see a picture of an ugly old woman. The picture doesn't change, what changes is how you *choose* to see it.

After that day in the hospital parking lot, I decided that ink drawing was a good metaphor for my life. I had always chosen to see whatever was bad, whatever was ugly about me. I knew my life was really great, but only if I *wanted* to see it that way. From then on, I chose to see the good.

It was slow going at first, but all I did was try to do a few little things to feel better about myself like joining a new club or taking walks every night after dinner. The momentum from those little victories kept me going and gave me the confidence to take on more things. Every day, in small ways, I began reshaping my life.

I started going to the gym and lost a ton of weight. When I'd pass a mirror, I'd stop to look at myself. I *never* used to do that before. On a recent trip with friends, we went hiking and I was in better shape than everyone else.

I also became more outgoing. When I would go out shopping, or whatever, I started talking to total strangers. I've been living with these new changes for several years now, and I can honestly say I've taken back control of my life.

Now I know what my needs are and I give myself positive reinforcement. *Cute, pretty, smart,* those are all of my fears, so I turn them around. Now I sell myself on the fact that I *am* all of those things. I am because I say that I am.

There's a long hallway in my house where I keep all of my family pictures. Every morning I stop and look at the picture of me taken when I was a little girl. I stand there for a moment and talk to her. I tell her she's pretty and smart. I tell her she can do or be anything she wants, and that she's loved.

When you look at your life, you can see the good or the bad. It's just as easy to see one as it is to see the other. Whenever I feel unsure of something, whenever I feel bad or think someone has slighted me, I try to see the pretty lady.

You must be the change you wish to see in the world.

Mahatma Gandhi (1869–1948)
Indian statesman and philosopher

 # The dancer
(Sharon, cashier, 34)

I always wanted to be a dancer. My parents didn't have much money and they couldn't afford dance lessons for me, but it didn't matter. Even without the lessons, I made dancing the focus of my life. I considered myself a dancer. That's how I saw myself.

My girlfriend across the street and I used to stay out late every day, just practicing. We watched all of those weekend dance shows on TV. We studied every music video that had dancing in it. It was all I thought about.

I only danced on stage once. It was for a high school talent show. I picked the music and choreographed my own routine. My parents were there, my neighbors were there. I was a nervous wreck, but when that music came up and it was just me out there on that stage . . . God, it was great. It was *really* great.

Right after the show was over, people just swarmed around me. Everybody said it was *amazing*. I never felt like that in my entire life.

For the first time, I felt like things were coming together for me. I felt like I could do anything.

A week or so after the show, I asked my parents if I could go live with my aunt in New York City. The idea was I could finish school there and begin to try to start dancing full-time. I even thought about trying out for the Julliard School of Fine Arts.

My parents thought it over for about a half a second and then said no. They said I was too young. They didn't like the fact I'd be living in New York City *and* living so far away from them. That was that.

It was around that time, at 16, I met my husband. We got married when I was 20 and I had my son at 21. The focus of my life switched from dancing to taking care of my kids, getting a night job and paying the bills. It's been stressful at times. The stress makes it a lot harder to quit these. *(She points to her lit cigarette.)*

Now that we've got two kids and two *very* busy work schedules, it's hard for me and my husband to find time. We go out dancing sometimes, maybe a couple of times a year, but not nearly as often as I'd like. It's fun when we do go out because people usually ask me if I'm a professional dancer. I like that.

People ask me if I'm bothered by the fact that I never became a dancer. I tell them no, it doesn't bother me. It's okay because I wouldn't have made it. Even if I *had* gone to live with my aunt in the city, it probably wouldn't have worked out. Something like a *thousand* people try out for every dancing job that opens up. My chances were one in a thousand. I'm sure I saved myself a lot of heartache, you know what I mean?

But to answer your question: yeah, I always wanted to be a dancer.

Glory is fleeting, but obscurity is forever.

Napoleon Bonaparte (1769–1821)
General, conqueror, and Emperor of France

If you're going to San Francisco...
(Barry, retired counselor, 61)

Everybody has different circles of friends. In one of my circles, my friends from the marina, a favorite topic is music and music trivia. When we get together, there's lots of talk about song titles, bands, musicians, and album covers. Because of our age group, most of the music that's discussed is from the '60s and '70s.

Among those friends, I'm the butt of a running joke. As much as I enjoy listening to these conversations about music, I can never participate. My friends are always amazed that I don't recognize certain songs or that I don't know the names of famous bands or musicians. They look at me as if I'm from another planet.

The reason I mention this is because it typifies what I missed out on when I was in my teens and twenties. I don't mean that my life stinks because I don't know music trivia; it's just an example of how I missed out on my youth. Whether it was getting my degree, getting a job, or taking care of my family, I was always too busy to stop and smell the roses.

When I was a kid, duty and hard work were held up as the most important things in life. As a result, I was never allowed to be young when I was young. There was just no time for it.

My parents were good people, but they had my whole life mapped out for me. They showed me all of the hurdles they wanted me to jump, and by the time I had cleared them all, I was living someone else's life. I had become who *they* wanted me to be.

One of the couples from the marina exemplifies everything I didn't do, but should have done. Dusty and his girlfriend Noreen took off after high school in a VW van and drove out to California. They were in San Francisco in the late '60s and early '70s, during the height of the whole Haight Ashbury scene.

Being there at that time, they witnessed one of the biggest cultural changes in this country's history. They spent a few years knocking around, meeting people, and experiencing new places and new things. They just went out there and lived life. They grew up, learned a lot, and now have quite a few amazing stories to tell.

When they came back from their adventure, Dusty went to college and became a teacher. He married Noreen, they had children, and they lived happily ever after. For them, it was just that simple.

They didn't throw their lives away by postponing their education. They don't wear signs around their necks now that say, "Hippie burn-out." They're normal, successful people. They lived, and no one can ever take that away from them.

Dusty and Noreen were adventurers, they were explorers. They had a wonderful experience, which I think greatly contributes to the development of a person. It's that kind of experience that helps a person discover who they are and what their needs are.

Pretty much anything you do or look for in life is predicated on how well you know yourself. Instead of approaching relationships, careers, lifestyles, etc., with some sense of ourselves, too many of us end up trying to field test who and what we are. We go out into the world and guess. We try to force fit ourselves into whatever our parents, our guidance counselors, or our culture demands of us. That sort of thing leads to a lot of heartbreak and angst.

If you have limited experiences, you'll make decisions based on those limited experiences. If you do that, you'll end up with a limited life. If you don't take the time early on in life to experience some of life's growing pains and discover yourself, then you'll be stuck trying to do it as an adult. *That's* difficult.

I know exactly what I'm talking about because I *did* that. I followed somebody else's plan. I stumbled along not knowing much about what I liked, what I wanted, or what I was good at. It's not a good plan for a happy life, I can tell you.

I'm a few years older than Dusty and Noreen, but we're in very similar places in our lives now. We live in similar neighborhoods, drive similar cars, and have generally the same type of lives. The only real difference between them and me is that *they had* their youth. *They had* their moments in the sun. Dusty and Noreen embraced their youth, and I ignored mine.

No Andy Warhol
(Abriti, advertising agency owner, 43)

When I was 18 years old, I returned home to India. Up until then, I had been attending a prestigious private school in the United States. Living as an independent young woman in American did not prepare me for the life that awaited me back home in Mumbai (*formerly Bombay*).

I returned home bubbling with an "I want to conquer the world" enthusiasm, but my parents had other plans for me. They thought I should conquer the marriage market and be the first one of my friends to the altar. Our ideas did not match.

My dream was to study further, go on to college, and become a computer graphics and animation specialist. No one was doing that in India at the time. I dreamt of being an innovator. I wanted to fulfill my creative desires in a rarified atmosphere. I wanted to be like Andy Warhol, a pioneer in my chosen field.

At first, I resisted my parents' ideas about marriage, but they enlisted the help of my entire family. I soon found myself battling all of my aunts, uncles, and 50 other close family members. I could have rebelled, but I was just out of high school and I was still inexperienced. Besides, I could *not* hurt my parents. Sentiments here are very different than they are in America. So that was it. I got married too young and couldn't go back to America to get the education that would have fulfilled my dreams.

My friends back in the U.S. were a bit sad and a little disappointed when I wrote to them and told them I would not be coming back. The letters they wrote me were full of stories about college and adventure and possibilities. I still have all of the letters they sent me that year.

That was many years ago. I love my family life, but I wish I could have just waited four short years before I got married. That's all I would have needed to start on the path toward my dreams.

The path I *did* take led me to start and run my own advertising agency, but there's nothing very innovative about it. Mine is just one of many agencies here in Mumbai. I am *no* Andy Warhol.

The path I took has left an unfulfilled wish in me.

Succinctly speaking
(Danny, project supervisor, 33)

If I could do it over again, I'd have gone out a lot more, but I'd have drank a lot less.

Baking in a boxcar
(Will, retired small business owner, 66)

I did really well in school when I was a kid. In fact, I did so well that I got a full scholarship to Brooklyn Tech. At the time, Brooklyn Tech was one of the best private high schools in New York City. It was known for its excellent engineering department.

It was during my sophomore year that I began to lose interest in the whole thing. The emphasis on engineering got to be too dull. By then, I had discovered beer and girls and I just didn't care about school anymore. After cutting too many classes, they finally kicked me out. I enrolled in public school, but dropped out shortly after that.

For the next two years, I worked a few "no responsibility" type jobs, just spinning my wheels. I'm not sure what I was thinking. I guess that's it. I *wasn't* thinking.

It was around that time my high school girlfriend dumped me. When I think about it now, I don't blame her. All I wanted to do was hang out at Jones Beach, drink beer, and raise hell. Not much of a future in that.

I was really thrown for a loop when she left me. I didn't know what to do next. They still had the draft back in the '50s, so instead of waiting around to be drafted, I joined the Army.

I don't know if it's the same today, but back then, the Army used to put people in what was called a "repo depot." It was a holding area where they kept us before we went to basic training. We were put there until there were enough of us to fill a basic training class.

It was in the repo depot that I had my eyes opened. The Army had us unloading boxcars all day in the *blazing* heat. While I sweated my butt off, I thought about the Brooklyn Tech scholarship I blew, the shot at college I ignored, and it really bothered me. I felt trapped.

I realized I had not been making any *real* choices for myself. I had been drifting. It was while I was baking in one of those boxcars that I knew I had to do something with my life.

Being in the Army showed me how important it was to have an education. In the 1950s, the Army was changing. It was becoming more modern and more technical. It used to be you could be illiterate and still be in the Army, but that all changed the year I joined.

I remember this one career sergeant; his name was Alden. Almost every day, I heard him telling the other career Army guys who were illiterate to get going and to take advantage of the schooling that the Army offered. He tried to help as many of those guys as he could because he knew they'd have to pass a literacy test when it came time for them to reenlist.

Despite his coaching, most of the illiterate guys in my company never learned to read. I'll never forget the looks on their faces when the Army refused to let them reenlist. The Army was their life. They had nowhere else to go.

Things kept happening to reinforce the new ideas I had about my choices and my life. I was really beginning to see there were some pretty harsh lessons to be learned out there. On a daily basis, I was getting ordered around by people who could barely read and write. It seemed like there were a lot of stupid people running the world.

Maybe I was naive, but it seemed to me all you needed was a piece of paper to put on the wall, a diploma, in order to get opportunity. If you wanted opportunity, you had to prepare for it. Without question, I knew I had to get my high school equivalency diploma and make plans to go to college as soon as I got out.

Saving for college became my top priority. Because the Army didn't pay much, I had to come up with a creative solution to solve my money problems. I started a slush fund.

Everywhere you turned in the Army, there were guys who were broke and looking to borrow money. I began to lend guys money at interest. There were only a few of us on base doing it, so business was good. By the time I got out, I had accumulated enough to pay for my first semester of college.

My discharge from the Army came a month too late for me to enroll in the fall semester. I did *not* want to waste time waiting around for the next semester to start; I had wasted too much time already. They had different enrollment rules for the evening classes, so I enrolled as a night student. It wasn't what I wanted, but it was the best I could do under the circumstances.

A good friend of mine heard I had to enroll as a night student and he came up with a really great idea. He said that I should go down there on whichever day the regular students went to sign up for their classes and just blend in. He said, "Just stand in line, show them the enrollment papers that you *do* have, and plead ignorance. Just tell them you signed up as a regular student and you received these 'night classes' forms. You don't have to tell them anything else. Just stand there and smile. They'll take care of you." He was right. After a few polite conversations with the ladies at the registrar's office, I was enrolled as a full-time day student.

After three years in the Army, there was a noticeable difference in my level of maturity as compared to my college classmates. There was one guy in particular who was in a lot of my classes. I can't remember his name, but I can still picture his face. This guy was always saying, "Hey, Will! We're all going to get drunk at this place on 8th Street. Do you want to come?!"

He was a nice guy, but I just couldn't relate to him. He was so excited to be going out drinking, you'd think he had just been released from prison or something. By then, I knew that there was a hell of a lot more in the world than drinking at three o'clock in the afternoon. I did that for three full years in the Army. That's all we did when the sun went down. Now, I had a job to get to. I had to pay tuition.

There were a few other guys like me around campus—returning students who had spent time in the armed services. We used to talk about the differences between us and most of the other students. I'm sure those younger classmates of ours thought we were snubbing them, but we weren't. We just couldn't identify with them. The other veterans and I were in college to get our degrees. That was it.

As an aside, by the end of the first semester—not the first year, but the first semester—that guy who always asked me to go drinking with him was thrown out of school for bad grades.

The most important thing I realized during my time in the Army, in college, and throughout the rest of my life for that matter is your life is really a series of choices. The choices you make create the life that you end up with. *Because* life is a series of choices, ultimately, you define yourself.

In the long run, we shape our lives, and we shape ourselves.
The process never ends until we die. And the choices
we make are ultimately our responsibility.

Eleanor Roosevelt (1884–1962)
Former First Lady of the United States

# An American in Florence
(Doug, entrepreneur/former airline pilot, 39)

I never had any interest in traveling to Europe. It's not like I thought I'd hate it or anything, I just never thought about it. All that changed a few years ago when my brother talked me and my wife into going to Portugal. *That* was amazing.

We stayed in the old part of Lisbon. With its Roman ruins, cobblestone streets, and amazing food, I thought I was in heaven. It was the most fun I've ever had with my pants on.

The success of our Portugal trip led to other trips. Next was Spain, then Italy. Our trip to Italy was fantastic. We had done some reading on the subject, and we decided to spend most of our time in Florence. It lived up to every expectation I had. It's got to be the most beautiful place I've ever seen.

Florence was the ignition point of the Renaissance. Leonardo Da Vinci, Michelangelo, Brunelleschi, Raffaello — all of their works are represented there. Seeing their sketches, inventions, sculptures, and paintings was a little intimidating. Those guys probably did more during one rainy Saturday afternoon in the 1400s than I'll do in my entire life.

I saw Galileo's telescopes at the science museum. *Galileo's telescopes.* I found if I bent over and shoved my head between the glass cases, I could look through one of them.

After I dislodged my head, I turned around and saw a shriveled relic in a bell jar. It was Galileo's middle finger preserved for posterity. It was like he caught me looking through his telescope and he was flipping me off from beyond the grave. Think about this for a second: That guy was so important, *they kept his finger*. Florence is the major leagues.

It wasn't just the artwork and the museums that made our Florence trip great; there was something else. One morning when my pregnant wife and I headed out to do our laundry, something sort of unusual happened. We were walking down the street when we heard the sound of English. We looked up and saw a small group of American kids walking towards us. From the small pieces of their conversation that we overheard, we knew that they were high school kids. As we got closer, we smiled and nodded. They smiled and nodded, and that was it; the moment passed.

I looked at them over my shoulder for a second or two, and I thought about what *I* was doing when I was their age. When I was in high school, I didn't *do* anything. My school environment was *not* good, and because of that, I totally withdrew. I didn't go to the prom, my picture isn't in the yearbook and I didn't even go to graduation. I spent my time sitting around, bored out of my mind, badmouthing my parents, complaining a lot, smoking dope, drinking, and otherwise doing nothing.

At the time, I thought I *was* doing something. That "Ha! *I'm* not in the yearbook" attitude of mine actually took some doing. It took a lot of hard work to be so disconnected from everything. The problem wasn't that I withdrew from a bad situation; the problem was that I didn't move towards any good situations. I should have *done* something. It was like I was just sitting in the corner pouting.

I was about 36 when we took our trip to Italy. It was purely by accident that I discovered what I loved doing. I loved to travel. I loved speaking Italian. I *loved* Florence. Why the hell did it take me so long to find these things out?

Don't get me wrong, I was very happy to be there at that stage of my life, but seeing those kids made me realize something. I saw it in an instant, in a flash. What if *I* had come here when I was in high school? What if I had started down this path sooner? If I had explored a little and tried a few things when *I* was 18, what kinds of adventures would I have had? Would I have tried to learn Italian? Would I have met Italian girls? Would the experience of seeing Florence when I was 18 have been even *more* amazing than it is now? If I had changed my life even just *a little* back then, what might the cumulative effects of those changes be today?

If you were flying a large jet across the country and you knew you wanted to fly around a mountain range 100 miles away, there are a few things you could do. While the mountains were still 100 miles off, you could make a small course correction: you could turn one degree to the left or right. Over time, that tiny, imperceptible course correction would keep you clear of those mountain peaks. If you waited until you were just a few miles away before you thought about turning, you'd have to turn ninety degrees to either side, grit your teeth, and pray you were going to make it.

If I had turned just one degree to the left when I was their age, where would it have taken me? Do you know what I mean? If you start to find out what's out there a bit earlier in life, then maybe *everything* comes a little easier.

When I walked past those high school kids on that street in Florence, I felt a sense of mourning. I mourned the fact that I had wasted those years of my life. I mourned the fact that I couldn't go back and change it. I mourned the fact that, for me, that ship had sailed.

Ever since that day, I constantly ask myself, *What will I mourn at age 50? At age 60? What am I going to regret having missed out on later in life?* That new way of looking at things has changed everything for me. When I lost my airline job after September 11, it gave me the vision and the guts to refinance my house and spend $100,000 of my own money pursuing my dream of becoming a successful entrepreneur. That one morning in Florence changed my life.

This isn't about what I think other kids or other people should do. I'm not looking for converts. This is about what I wish *I* had done differently. If I could somehow go back and talk to myself when I was 18 I'd say, "Stop wasting your time. You're having a tough time right now. I understand that, but do something about it. You could be in *Florence*."

Decisive moments
(Tim, law enforcement officer, 38)

My tough time came when I got out of high school. I was completely unprepared for adulthood. My parents had raised me to be a kid for the first 17 years, 11 months, and 29 days of my life, but the day I turned 18, I was expected to be an adult. Like the flip of a switch, I was held fully responsible for my bills, my future, my life—everything. It was a tough transition. It made starting college pretty difficult.

My older brother had what you might call an interesting college experience. He got a girl pregnant and ended up dropping out. Because of his bad track record at college, my parents weren't very supportive when it came time for me to go. I guess you could say I had no brass ring to go for.

The best I could manage was going to a local college. I went for less than two years before I stopped. My grades weren't great, so I took a year off from school and started working.

I knocked around for a year, working part-time in more than a few bad jobs. I saw my co-workers, the people who had been working in those bad jobs for years, and I didn't like what I saw. They complained *constantly*. They seemed like angry people with no future. They looked and acted like they were having miserable lives.

Then I realized that the only difference between me and them was time. If I stayed there, I would become just like them. That scared the hell out of me.

It was obvious that if I didn't change what I was doing, all I could look forward to was more of the same. I was about 20 when the light bulb finally came on. I told myself I was *not* going to have a crappy life. It was time to get my act together.

That was a turning point for me. From then on, I focused on providing a future for myself. The first thing I felt I had to do was get a college degree. I returned to school with a new attitude. I was there to succeed, not just to drift from high school to the "next logical step." I took that momentum and carried it through everything I've done since.

I finally figured out there's a point in your life when you realize it's *your life*. Sooner or later, something opens your eyes to the fact that you either have the life you want or the life you don't want. When that day comes, you either accept who and what you are, or you say no and try to do something about it.

Nobody ever explained that to me. My parents *never* said those things. I wish they had. To be fair, you can't make someone else's light bulb come on for them, but you *can* help them to be ready when it does. That's why I discuss these sorts of things with my kids.

I tell my son, "Life-changing experiences are the things that change your life." What I mean by that is some things in life are seminal experiences. You know, decisive moments. How you react to those things controls where your life goes. You can either go down the tubes or up to great heights.

People who are never lost or never go through any uncertain times in their life probably won't know what to do when life's first speed bump comes along. I think you *need* to struggle and wander sometimes. Negative experiences can give you some perspective and some humility. There is no shame in learning from your mistakes. You've just got to keep moving.

Realizing that your future is up to you can be a scary thing, but it's also very liberating. There's a lot of freedom there. Whether you feel scared or liberated doesn't really matter. What matters is whether or not you recognize it in the first place. What matters is whether or not you act.

Christmas morning
(Anthony, retired NYC police officer, 74)

If I could go back and change something about my life, I'd change how closed-minded I was as a young man. That would have opened up so much for me. Instead, I was a little bit of a wise guy growing up.

The biggest change I wish I could have made earlier was how I felt about black and Hispanic people. As a white kid growing up on Southern Boulevard in the Bronx, I didn't like black people. I didn't *know* any black people, but I still didn't like them. Everybody in my neighborhood was like that back then. It's how people were raised. Being a cop changed me.

When I was brand new on the job, I was partnered up with some wonderful black officers. Theses guys were World War II veterans *and* they already had eight or ten years on the job. I was *in awe* of those guys.

In between calls, we'd sit in the car with a coffee and Danish, just talking. We got along great and there was a lot of mutual respect. They showed me the ropes and looked out for me. They could not have been nicer.

My precinct house just so happened to be in the neighborhood where I grew up, but before I became a cop, I never knew there was life outside of my tiny area. Being on the job, we saw *all* sorts of neighborhoods. There were the black areas, the Italian area over on Arthur Avenue, Hispanic, Jewish, Irish — everything. Going into people's houses, seeing them when they were sick, helping them with their problems, you got to see that everybody is the same. The rest doesn't matter.

The thing that changed my mind the most was a maternity call we got from somewhere near Brook Avenue, which was mostly a black area. This was early Christmas morning in 1955, when I was brand new on the job. When we got up to that apartment, the baby had already been born, but there was still a lot of cleaning up to be done. My partner went down to the car to radio for an ambulance and left me to take care of the situation.

I didn't know what to do. We were trained to use our pinky fingers to help clear out the baby's mouth, which I did, but I had never seen or done anything like that before. I was a *wreck*.

Luckily there were several other black ladies from around the apartment building who were there to help. They were so caring, so calm, and so matter-of-fact about how they handled the whole situation. They handled *me* the same way.

They saw how shook up I was and they kidded with me. "Oh, we've got a young cop here! Is this your first delivery? You're doing great." They said things like that to me the whole time I was there.

They sat me down, gave me some coffee, and we sort of had ourselves a nice Christmas morning together. One of the ladies even stood next to me with her hand on my shoulder, trying to make *me* feel at ease. The love those women had for the new mother, the baby, and for me was really something. They reminded me of the ladies in *my* family.

People always like to say that folks from black and Hispanic neighborhoods hate the police. Well, that's a lie. The people in my area knew me. When they saw me, they waved to me. Whenever one of us cops would get into trouble, they were always there for us.

This was years before the walkie talkie and we had no way to radio for help if we were away from the car. Plenty of times when I would be wrestling around in the street with someone, the neighborhood people watched out for me. Phone calls were made; backup arrived. Those were good and decent people.

There was so much I didn't know when I was a young man. I'm glad I had the chance to learn something. I don't think everybody gets that same chance. I just wish it could have happened sooner.

 ## Making her own way
(Arlene, retired elementary school teacher, 59)

When I was a young girl, I dreamt of traveling the world. My family didn't have a lot of money, so we never went anywhere. I just kept postponing my dreams, sitting on them and waiting for something to happen. By the time I was 24 years old, I had decided to do something about it.

I had been working as a teacher for a few years, but I still didn't have enough money saved to travel overseas. Even if I *had* the money, I knew the next obstacle I would have to overcome would be the fact that I had been leading such a sheltered life. I was still living with my parents and had never lived on my own. I knew I'd have to overcome a few of my fears before I could live my dream of traveling the world.

My desire to travel eventually took over and I began to look for solutions to both my money and my independence problems. I came up with an idea that was absolutely perfect. I applied to become a teacher for the DOD, the Department of Defense.

If accepted, it meant I would live overseas and teach American children whose parents were in the Armed Forces. The DOD would supply me with free food, shelter, transportation, etc. It seemed like a great way to transition from living with my parents to living on my own. Working abroad for the DOD, I could travel extensively without being completely by myself. It was perfect.

When I received word that I had been accepted by the DOD, I

resigned my civilian teaching position and took a teaching job with the U.S. Army. The Army has bases all over the world, but you don't get to choose where you're going. You go wherever they need you. They offered me Puerto Rico or the Philippines. I chose the Philippines. It sounded more exotic than Puerto Rico. Besides, I knew I'd get to travel on my days off and Asia seemed like a great place to start.

It was raining like *crazy* the first night I arrived in the Philippines. It was right in the middle of typhoon season. The weather was so bad that several of the local roads had washed out.

The driver who picked me up from the airport spoke almost no English and drove like a maniac. He almost went off the road *three times*. I was yelling, he was yelling. What a welcome.

When they brought me to my living quarters, I was shocked by the conditions. Because of the incredible humidity, everything smelled moldy. The beds smelled. The sheets, the mattresses, the pillows— *everything* had that mildew smell. There were special lights in all of the closets just to dry out the mildew.

I was not used to any of it. I felt homesick and out of place. I thought I had made a huge mistake. I *cried* that first night.

All of those feeling vanished in a day or so. After I met all of the other teachers, I knew I had made a great decision. They were *wonderful*. They came from all over the United States and all over the world. Soon, I felt at ease and I felt as if I belonged.

For the first time in my life, I was out on my own. It was up to me to make new friends. It was my first experience with having a room-mate too. It was wonderful.

Whenever the other teachers and I had a few days off, we would travel all throughout Southeast Asia. I got to see Taiwan, Hong Kong, Thailand, Singapore, and Cambodia. All of this took place in about 1968, right when the Vietnam War was going on. It made the traveling a bit tense at times, but we always had fun.

During a Christmas break one year, we traveled to Cambodia. No matter where we went in that country, we got funny looks from all of the locals. We just thought they were being rude to us, but meanwhile, the U.S. was *bombing Cambodia at night.* None of us found out about that until much later on. No wonder they were looking at us funny. God, we could have been killed too!

My next assignment was Germany. Just like before, my fellow teachers and I took every opportunity to travel. The only places in Europe I *didn't* see were the Scandinavian countries. Other than those places, we saw every major city and attraction in Europe. It was fantastic.

The Cold War was at its height back then and I saw some pretty scary things during my time in Germany. One night, my roommate and I were traveling through East Germany by train when our train made an unscheduled stop outside one of the stations. On the next track, another train came to a stop alongside of us. The other train had its interior lights on, so we could see everything going on inside.

All of a sudden, we saw East German police working their way through the other train. There were soldiers too, guys with machine guns, looking for something or someone. It didn't take long for them to find who they were looking for.

Right across from my window, I saw them roust an old lady. They made her dig through her bag for a second or two and then they took her off of the train. And I mean *they took her off of the train!* Her feet didn't even touch the ground. In those days, that sort of thing was common in that part of Europe.

My time as an Army teacher for the DOD lasted three years. Those three years were really amazing. I went from being a sheltered young woman to a world traveler almost overnight.

Living in those countries made all of the difference. It allowed me to experience things not as a tourist, but as a local. I was really able to absorb the culture wherever I went. It was incredibly empowering. I'm really glad I did it. I'm proud of myself.

I dream my painting and then paint my dream.

Vincent Van Gogh (1853 –1890)
Dutch artist

A whisper and the Dark Continent

A few weeks after my twenty-second birthday, my next door neighbors returned from a month-long safari in east Africa. Along with their two kids, they had traveled hundreds of miles across Kenya and Tanzania in a canvas-topped four-wheel-drive vehicle. They camped along the way, seeing all of the incredible beauty of equatorial Africa.

They very graciously spent hours with me, reliving every aspect of their trip. It was beyond belief. I was fascinated by all of it.

Ordinarily a trip like that would interest me, but in the end, I would find some reason not to go. In the past, there would have always been some fear or excuse holding me back, but as I looked at my neighbor's pictures and listened to their amazing stories, a new and strange spirit seemed to be taking hold of me. I became more afraid of *not* going, of regretting it years later. I put "Go on an African safari" on my life list and ignored my fears.

After making a few inquiries, I thought I might be able to afford a similar trip. The price was steep, but I felt the price of regret would be much higher. I immediately began saving my money, and for over a year, I bought nothing but essential items. My parents, who had always been a source of encouragement, saw the change in me and offered to pay for a portion of the trip. Fifteen months later, they were dropping me off at one of the international departure terminals at JFK Airport.

Despite all of my big plans and big talk, I was still very much afraid. There I was, about to go to Africa on a three-week safari *alone*. Sure, I would be meeting up with other travelers once I had arrived in

Tanzania, but I had never done anything like this before. In addition, the people with whom I would be traveling were total strangers. What if there was trouble? What if I got lost? My mind raced as I began to wonder just what I had gotten myself into.

My fears began to fade the moment I arrived in Arusha, Tanzania. The natural beauty of the country was beyond description. The way the air smelled, the look of the acacia trees, the sight of Mount Kilimanjaro in the distance all served to calm me and excite me at the same time.

Most of the three-week trip was spent moving slowly west across the Serengeti plains. Every evening at dusk, we would stop our large canvas-topped truck in a suitable area and set up our campsite. Once a week we would spend the night in whatever lodge was along our route, but other than that we were completely on our own. It was a great feeling.

One of the best things we did while in Tanzania was camp inside the Ngorongoro crater. It is about 2,000 feet deep and 14 miles across at its widest point. The variety of wildlife and the beauty of the area were unbelievable. Every day at sunrise, we would look towards the distant rim of the crater and watch as the morning mist curled over the edge like a wave trying to flood the basin, only to see it evaporate before it reached the bottom. We stayed in that amazing place for four days.

We continued our westward push across the Serengeti, seeing animals of every description. We saw water buffalos, zebras, and gazelles. We saw lions, cheetahs, and hyenas. We were charged by elephants, menaced by a rhino, and chased by ostriches.

Just when we thought the trip could not get any more beautiful or spectacular, we arrived at our base camp in the Virunga Mountains of Rwanda. With its rugged mist-covered mountains and its lush rainforests, it was what I had always dreamed Africa would look like. It was there that we began to prepare for our gorilla climb.

Three other tourists and I were chosen to visit a special group of gorillas. The only way to do that was to spend the night deep in the mountains, at altitude, in order to be able to find the gorillas first thing in the morning. Accompanied by our cook and a local guide, we left the others behind at base camp and set off up the mountain to find our campsite. We hiked up those slippery slopes in the rain for hours, stumbling over wet rocks and moss-covered logs. At dusk, we finally reached the dirt-floored, corrugated steel shack where we would spend the night.

The next morning, because of our perfect starting point, it wasn't long before we were sitting among that special group of mountain gorillas. It was an amazing experience. Their size, their musky smell, the way they gently interacted with us—it was all so unbelievable.

I came within three feet of one of the adolescent females. It's a cliché, but their eyes really did have an amazing "human-like" quality. It seemed our time with them passed in the blink of an eye.

After hiking back down the mountain for a few hours, we rested in the grass in a local village and waited for our ride back to base camp. As I lay there, I could not stop smiling. There I was, lying in the grass in a small Rwandan village at the base of the Virunga Mountains. I had just spent an hour among a troop of gorillas. I had just finished a three-week safari covering several hundred miles of equatorial Africa. I had been afraid to do *all* of it, but I did it anyway. It was an indescribable feeling.

Looking back on the entire experience, I feel blessed. Going on that trip was like pushing over the first domino in a line of a thousand dominos. It truly started the rest of my life in motion. Had it not been for that simple decision to go, to conquer my fear, I never would have experienced any of it. Because of that one decision, I saw Africa. I climbed mountains and fought off giant rats. I met Masi warriors. I ate warthog.

All of those experiences were truly unforgettable, but the most memorable thing that happened to me in Africa took place early one evening when we stopped to make camp somewhere in the Serengeti. The other travelers and I were making idle conversation while standing on the food line. It was dusk.

Some of the other travelers wanted to know more about me. They asked me where I was from, what I did for a living, that sort of thing. Finally, one of them asked me how old I was.

At 23 years of age, I was at least 15 years younger than the next youngest person on the trip. In fact, most of the other travelers were well in their fifties and a few were in their sixties. When I told them my age, many of them simply shook their heads and repeated the number as if in disbelief. Just then, one of the travelers turned to the person next to him and said, "Can you imagine having these experiences at *his* age?"

If I live to be a hundred years old, I'll never forget that moment. I smiled and I knew, *really* knew, for the first time in my life that the future was mine to guide and control. And as I looked around and saw the Serengeti Plain disappearing with the fading light, I thought of the whisper. I thought about how its kind and delicate sound had changed my life, and I was grateful.

Life is either a daring adventure or nothing.

Helen Keller (1880–1968)
American author, speaker, and activist

The One Who Got Away

*Footfalls echo in the memory down the
passage which we did not take, towards the
door we never opened into the rose garden.*

T. S. Eliot (1888–1965)
American poet

Wearing a white dress

It can be the smallest of things, the most fleeting of moments that stay with someone.

There's a scene from the film classic *Citizen Kane*, in which an older man describes to a younger man just how strange a person's memory can be. The older man begins by telling the younger man that he might not be able to appreciate the story he's about to hear. He tells him, "You're pretty young, Mr. Thompson. A fellow will remember a lot of things you wouldn't think he'd remember."

The older man goes on to tell a story about how he, many years ago, stood on the deck of a ferry boat. Passing in the opposite direction was another ferry. Standing on the deck of that other ferry was the most beautiful woman he had ever seen. She was a vision . . . wearing a white dress. The man went on to say that although he saw her only once, and well over 50 years had passed, not a month went by that he did not think of her.

Many people I know still remember that scene. They remember it because of its power: the perfect and sometimes terrible truth of it. Many of us carry moments like that around with us our entire lives. Not just a mere glimpse of a girl on a ferry boat, but stronger ones, real ones.

And unlike some film character who fondly remembered a girl who drifted by wearing a white dress, our real moments are not always looked back upon so casually. That's because our moments are usually times when we *had* control, but failed to act. The young woman you never asked to dance, the boy in college you were crazy about, but let slip away; those are the types of moments that seem to come back to haunt us when the house is quiet.

That's one of the reasons I asked my interviewees about this subject. If we knew just how bothered we were going to be tomorrow by the romantic chances we didn't take today, perhaps we would decide to take more of them.

The stories we tell about "the one who got away" can be very biting because they often point out our character flaws (timidity, lack of self-worth, procrastination). And sometimes, worse still, they expose our illusions.

One of the first formal interviews I did was with a gentleman who was an accountant. When I contacted him for an interview, he seemed interested, but he wanted to know more about the questions I would ask before he would agree. After we discussed several of the topics and questions covered by my standard interview, the one question that seemed to pique his interest was, "Do you have a story about the one who got away?" I explained to him that I wanted to know if he was bothered by the memory of a romance or a romantic opportunity he had let slip away.

Days later when the accountant and I finally sat down to begin the interview, he handed me a piece of paper. There were 41 names or place names written on it, each with a date placed next to it. "Sally Jones," "girl in history class," and "girl on line at the supermarket" were some of the things listed on his neatly typed page. In addition to the names and their associated dates, I noticed that 11 of the 41 entries were underlined in black. He said the list represented all of his missed romantic opportunities, and the underlined entries represented real regrets.

Not knowing what to make of his list, I looked at it and wondered where to begin. I asked him to tell me which one of the underlined entries bothered him the most. Without a moment's hesitation he said, "The girl at the dorm bus stop." The following is that story.

Underlined in black
(Phil, accountant, 43)

When I was 20 years old, I transferred to a state university. I had been there only about two months when I met an amazing girl. We were both standing at one of the dorm bus stops waiting for the morning bus to class.

It's been over 23 years, but I remember exactly what she looked like. She had sparkling blue eyes, dirty blonde hair, and a perfect "girl next door" quality. She was *beautiful*.

I can't remember who started it, but we began talking. We seemed to hit it off right away. This was great because I never had *any* rapport with women.

The bus pulled up and we got on. I didn't have the nerve to sit next to her, so I sat down near her. Despite my success at the bus stop, I completely froze up on the bus. Although I said nothing, I couldn't stop staring at her.

As luck would have it, we got off the bus at the same stop. She walked off in a different direction than I needed to go, but I walked behind her for a while, hoping that I could get up the courage to say something. My mind raced as I thought of what I should do next.

I was only a step behind her, when suddenly she slipped on the icy path. Like a scene right out of a movie, I was right there to catch her! I grabbed her under the arm and kept her from falling. She looked up at me with the most amazing smile.

She thanked me profusely, and I felt an amazing chemistry between us. She seemed to go out of her way to keep the conversation going. It was as if she was really trying to show me something of herself. We stood there for a moment or two and then she said, "Well, I hope to see you again soon," and walked away. Like an idiot, I let her go without getting her name or anything.

About three days later, *there she was.* She was standing at the same dorm bus stop as before. For whatever reason, I felt charged with confidence. We began speaking and things were going great. I said something like, "I promise if you fall again, I'll be right there to catch you!" She laughed as we relived the accident. It was all so perfect. It was like I was someone else: confident, funny, and charming.

When the bus arrived we both got on, but I froze up again. I didn't have the nerve to sit next to her. I just couldn't bring myself to do it, so I sat across the aisle two rows behind her.

She looked over at me a few times, but the confidence I felt earlier was gone. The "old" me was back, and I just couldn't make myself do or say the things I wanted to. I was saying to myself, "I can't go any further than this. She's so beautiful. She's so nice. If she gets to know me better, she's going to see that I'm not good enough for her. I've got no car, no money. I've got absolutely no experience with women. I'm nobody." That's *exactly* how I felt about myself back then. It was all part of the self-defeating attitude that I carried with me all through my twenties.

Eventually, we arrived at my stop. I got up and began to walk off the bus. She looked up at me and smiled as I walked by, but I said nothing. The moment passed and I found myself standing on the sidewalk watching the bus drive away. I never saw her again.

Of all of the names and all the things written down on my list, she's the one I still think about. She's the one that still bothers me. Maybe it wouldn't have gone anywhere and maybe it was all in my head, but she seemed to be taken with me right away and I blew it. I never had a college girlfriend; maybe she could have been mine. Maybe she could have been a lot of things.

I've never forgotten that mistake. I've thought a little bit about it here and there for all these years. It took me a very long time, but I eventually got to the point where I was able to learn from it and use it.

I learned to be less afraid and take advantage of opportunities. I learned to take a few emotional risks too. The thing is this: there was no reason for me to be so hard on myself back then for feeling self-conscious. A lot of people around me were probably feeling the same way.

Any of the successes I've had with women since then, including meeting my wife, are all because of what that one mistake taught me. Anytime I began to freeze up when I approached a woman, the thought of that girl in college and what I probably missed out on gave me the incentive to follow through. When push came to shove, I just didn't want to end up with my whole life being underlined in black. I learned who I *didn't* want to be from that girl at the dorm bus stop.

Seize the day; put no trust in the morrow!

Horace (65–8 B.C.)
Greek poet

 # Good girl, bad girl
(Amy, flight attendant, 48)

My first love and I grew up in the same town. Things between us started out slowly, just talking at first, and then we began dating regularly. I was 21 when we first got together and he was about 26. I really loved him.

He would invite me over his place for romantic dinners. He'd set the table with candles and flowers, but whenever he would ask me to stay the night, I'd always say no. I wanted us to have a physical relationship, but I played a lot of games with him when it came to sex. It was kind of a power trip for me. He wanted me, and as long as he did, I was in control. It didn't matter how much I loved him, how romantic he was, or how long we were together, I just kept shutting him down sexually.

I loved my guy desperately and I thought that meant I should play hard to get. I thought I could get him to marry me by being the "good girl." I ended up denying the strong sexual attraction I had for him in order to *be* the good girl.

I thought you acted one way around the guys you dated, and another way around the *one* guy you dated and *wanted to marry*. The whole thing was ridiculous because I was pretending to be somebody I wasn't. Let me tell you, I was *not* a nun. I really wanted him, but I thought the rules were the rules, so I played the part.

Remember, we are *not* talking about kids here. I was an adult. I was a 21-year-old woman at the start of our two-year relationship, but I still felt that I had to play the "good girl" game with him. Eventually he lost interest and walked away. That totally broke my heart. He was the *only* man to ever break my heart.

The worst thing about all of this is a couple of years after he left, he went out and married a girl who looks just like me. I see her around every once in a while. Whenever I see her I think, *That should have been me.*

About once every three years, I run into my old flame. The last time was on a rainy night when I was driving through a neighboring town. I was lost, so I stopped a jogger to ask for directions. *It was him.* Can you believe it? He seemed so happy to see me. God, he looked good.

For me, there's still an attraction there. I think it's there for him too, but it's something we've never explored. Whenever I see him I think, *If only.* Whenever I drive past a place we used to go or hear a song we used to like, I have the same sort of feeling. I have a lot of those "if only" type of moments when it comes to him.

Our relationship ended over 25 years ago, but I still find myself thinking about him a lot. Look, I am *not* saying I should have done something against my conscience or beliefs just to get some guy. That's the whole point. I went against what I was feeling and against what I really wanted to do because of some stupid idea about what I thought *he* wanted in a woman. It was just ignorance.

If I could do it all over again, I would *not* have played any games. I would have showed him how I felt about him physically, as well as with words. I was a grown woman back then. Who was I pretending to be anyway? All of that good girl/bad girl stuff is such a bunch of crap. I should have just been myself.

This above all: to thine own self be true,
and it must follow, as the night the day,
thou canst not then be false to any man.

William Shakespeare (1564–1616)
English playwright and poet

 Sitting on my hands
(Ron, technician, 39)

In the summer of 1991, I met a woman named Sara. I had just moved out to Chicago, and she was the manager of my new apartment complex. She was the first real friend I had when I moved out here.

Even though she was married, I kind of liked her right away. She had sort of a crooked smile, and a great laugh. She was smart, beautiful, and hard-working. She was a great mother to a great kid. She had it all.

We seemed to hit it off right from the start. Sometimes she'd ask me to take her to the movies on the nights her husband was working. Those were fun nights, but I was always a gentleman. I never touched her.

Sara started coming over to my apartment all the time. We'd sit around and have incredibly honest conversations about ourselves.

Because she was married, I felt I could tell her things about my social life that I couldn't tell other women. I told her about all of my past relationships and my heartbreaks. I told her about my difficulty in meeting women.

We talked about lots of things, but Sara seemed to want to talk about her marriage the most. The way Sara described it, she was in a bad marriage. She complained about her husband *constantly*. She'd even say things like, "I think my husband wants to leave me." It seemed to her that they were a mismatch and they had made a big mistake by getting married.

I never understood why she told me all that. I could never tell if she was doing it because we were friends, or if she was trying to see what my reaction would be. Regardless, I sat on my hands and I waited for her to clearly state her intentions.

I wanted to be with her romantically, but she was married and I couldn't bring myself to do anything about it. I came from a broken home. Divorce *ruined* my childhood. There was just no way that I could do that to someone else's family. If she said to me that she was going to leave her husband, *then* I'd tell her how I felt about her. *Then* it would be okay. At least that's how I thought I'd handle it.

For eight years, I waited for her to make her move. During those years, I never told Sara how I felt about her. Not once.

One day, Sara told me that she had just signed divorce papers. I was thrilled. I thought about how and when I would tell her my feelings, but I also continued to wait. There was always some excuse not to tell her how I felt, and I used every one of them. The truth is I didn't know what to do or say. I thought it to death. This went on for six months.

Sara called one afternoon and said she had some news. She said she had just met some guy and he had asked her out. I pretended to be happy for her, but I was really hurt. I said, "Hey, good luck with that," and hung up the phone.

I don't remember how long it took, but Sara ended up marrying that guy. I still can't believe it. It's *my story* and even *I* can't believe it.

Sara's been remarried for about two years. We talk from time to time, but it's different now. It's more casual. It's more superficial.

I still carry my secret feelings for her around with me, but so what? If you think about it, what difference does that make now? Because I never told her how I felt, it's like I never even loved her at all.

Looking back, I have this to regret,
that too often when I loved, I did not say so.

David Grayson (1890–1990)
American author

The faceless man
(Vicki, real estate agent, 26)

When I was about 20, I visited the island of Martha's Vineyard. A girl-friend of mine, her mother, and I went for the day. I was still in college at the time.

I had never been there before and I *loved* it. The beautiful ocean-front homes, the beaches, the clothing stores—it was great. We rented scooters and drove all over the island. We tried to see and do it all that day.

We were wandering around in some store when the strangest thing happened. In walked a guy who I had never seen before, and it was like I was struck by lightning. He looked *right at me*. Our eyes only met for an instant, but I had this amazing feeling about him. I can't describe it. It was like what you hear about when people describe "soul mates." Something came over me. He wasn't incredibly gorgeous or anything, but I felt an instant attraction.

A couple of seconds later, my friend came over and pulled me out of the store to go do something else, but I told her we had to go back in there. I *had* to meet that guy. We walked back into the store, but I didn't see him anywhere.

The weirdest part of the whole thing was I never really saw his face. It was his eyes I saw. He had blue eyes. I remember looking right at him, but I can't tell you what he looks like. Even as I was frantically looking through that store for him, I wasn't sure what he looked like! All I remembered was what he had on. He was wearing khaki shorts, a sweatshirt, and a baseball hat.

We spent the rest of the day looking all over the island for him. My girlfriend had the patience of a saint because I drove her crazy. I kept saying, "We have to find him! We have to find him!" but we never did.

Even though it was six years ago, I still think about him. I think about him *a lot*. I've even dreamt about him. Anytime I see one of those movies about fate or destiny, my mind wanders back to that day on Martha's Vineyard. I know it's weird, but I've thought about going back there just to look for him.

That guy on Martha's Vineyard was my "F.M.," as I call it. He was my "Faceless Man." That's the name I've given to a theory I have about women. The same theory goes for guys too, but it's so much truer for women.

A lot of women fantasize about a faceless man. They give him a job, a lifestyle, a body, personality traits, etc., but they don't give him a face. I think women do this so they can fit the next guy who comes along into the role of their perfect fantasy man. It's a way for women to fantasize, but also keep their options open at the same time.

When we reach puberty, we begin to form a picture in our minds of the type of guy we want. The older we get, the clearer the image gets. Since I was about 12 years old, I've been thinking about my F.M.

I've thought about who he'd be and what he'd do. I've seen us together a thousand times. We've held hands, we've kissed, and we've made love, but I've never seen his face. Not once.

Fantasizing about a faceless man is both good and bad. It's good to know what you want and it's good to have standards, but the whole F.M. thing can also be bad because your mind can get locked on an unrealistic model. Most likely, the *perfect* person doesn't exist. If you get stuck on that image, you'll waste a lot of time looking for it. Maybe that's what's happened to me.

My social life is pretty much nonexistent nowadays. My job and the hours I keep don't make it easy to meet guys. The heavy work schedule isn't so bad because staying busy is the only thing that keeps me from dwelling on my lack of a social life. Sounds like a trap, right?

The fact that I have such strong feelings for the guy I saw on Martha's Vineyard doesn't make any sense, but that's one of the reasons why it still stays with me. I never felt that way before and I haven't since. That's what makes me think that there might be something to it.

Sometimes I try to push all of those "soul mate" thoughts out of my head. Believing in those sorts of things is painless when there's nothing at stake, but if I start to believe it now, it really stings. I say that because sometimes I feel as if that guy on Martha's Vineyard *was* my soul mate. And if he was, then I missed my chance.

I'd give anything just to be able to have talked to him. Maybe he would have turned out to be rude or unavailable, but he might also have been the love of my life. I'll probably never know.

The truly educated person is
that rare individual who can
separate reality from illusion.

Author unknown

Did Pete call?
(Lynne, freelance photographer, 36)

Twenty-two years ago, I began a relationship with a guy named Pete. We met when our families rented cottages along a lake in New Hampshire one summer. I was 14 and he was 15. We hit it off right away.

At the end of the season, we didn't exchange numbers. It was the first relationship for both of us and we didn't know how to handle it. I thought, *Well, that's it.*

I was heartbroken because I had no way to reach him. Sure enough, when we went back to the lake the next summer, he and his family were there. I thought, *Oh, this is too good!*

We hit it off again and had a great time. It was all very young and innocent. At the end of the week, we exchanged addresses and made plans to correspond. We were pen pals all winter.

Sometime that winter, we found out our parents had booked different weeks for the upcoming summer. I told Pete which week my parents had booked and we agreed he should push his folks into booking the same week. We were sort of co-conspirators. It worked. I never told my mother until years later.

Our relationship went on for several years, all through high school. The fourth and last summer at the lake was when I was 17 and Pete was 18. We had a great time, but maybe something was wrong. Maybe it was too much too soon, I don't know.

Just like every other year, we made plans to correspond, but it didn't quite happen. He wrote for a while, but I got busy with my senior year in high school and we lost touch. We both got busy with life. Then it got to the point where too much time had passed for me to reach out to him. It felt weird. I felt like I couldn't just jump back in.

Then after two years, out of the blue I got a call from Pete. Well, I didn't get the call, but my brother did. I remember exactly where I was and what I was doing when I got the message. I was *thrilled*. It absolutely floored me.

My brother said, "You'll never guess who called." He knew what Pete meant to me and I figured he was teasing. I said, "You had better not be joking around!" I was really amazed. I couldn't believe how excited I was that he had called. I returned the call, but Pete wasn't there. I spoke to *his* brother briefly, but that was it.

Pete never got back to me. I didn't think of it at the time, but I just assumed Pete's brother gave him the message. My brother gave me *Pete's* message, so I naturally assumed that Pete's brother would do the same. Maybe that was a mistake.

Not only did I assume that Pete's brother gave him the message, I also assumed Pete's call was sort of a casual thing. Two years is a long time, right? I figured that he was just calling me on a whim. The fact that I never heard from him again kind of reinforced that idea.

A couple of years later, one of my girlfriends said, "You know, it took guts for him to call you out of the blue after two years. Think about it. He still had your number. He still knew where to find you. There was something there and all you did was call him back *once?*" As soon as she said it, I knew she was right. But by that time, Pete and his family had moved and there was no way for me to reach him.

Pete's always been on my mind, but some strange coincidences lately have really revived those old memories. A month ago, my friends and I were having a conversation about relationships and the guys in our lives that slipped away, which reminded me of him. Just yesterday, I was in line at the bank behind a woman who had the exact same last name as Pete. She wasn't related to him; I asked.

Three months ago, there was a story in one of the papers here in Boston that reminded me of him. The headline said, "Looking for Lynne." I grabbed it and read it, thinking it might be about how Pete was looking for me or something, but it wasn't about him . . . or me.

Now today, you're asking me these interview questions, which have me talking about him. It's really strange.

"What ever happened to Pete?" That's always been an unanswered question for me. Part of me really wants to know, but part of me doesn't. I don't want to hear that he's married and has six kids, you know what I mean? That might be too much to take.

If all of that stuff with Pete happened today, I would handle it a lot differently. If I had known this one guy and this one phone call would still be under my skin 17 years later, I would have left nothing up to chance. I would have been more proactive. I wouldn't have let a good one slip away.

Six weeks after conducting this interview, the following letter was sent to my publisher.

Mr. Green,

I just wanted to give you an update since my recent interview for your book. I thought about Pete after our chat, and I knew that I needed an answer of some sort. So, I found him on one of those classmate websites. I sent him an email and received a response nine minutes later!

We have been in daily contact for the last 18 days, and we are now dating!!!

Thank you for helping Pete and me reunite after many, many years. These events have been the best surprise of my life. I'll keep you posted . . .

Regards,
Lynne D.

P.S. Best wishes with your book.

Destiny is not a matter of chance;
it is a matter of choice.
It is not a thing to be waited for;
it is a thing to be achieved.

William Jennings Bryan (1860–1925)
Speaker, lawyer, and three-time U.S. presidential candidate

Hoping he'd turn around
(Sheri, administrative assistant, 25)

It was about four years ago, in the fall. I was walking along at an outdoor mall in Forest Hills, just doing some shopping to cheer myself up. It was during my junior year at St. John's University and I was working pretty hard.

I remember being pretty tired. I had no make-up on, my hair was in a ponytail, and I was wearing a pair of jeans and an old jacket. I was *not* dressed to impress.

All of a sudden, this guy taps me on the shoulder. He said, "Excuse me, do you know where the gym is?" Oh my God, that guy was *gorgeous*. He had a twinkle in his eye and one of those amazing perfect smiles.

I'm not shy at all, but that guy completely paralyzed me. All I could do was smile back at him and point over my shoulder towards where I *thought* the gym was. I was mush.

He laughed and said he really didn't want to know where the gym was. He said, "You're so pretty. I just wanted to talk to you and hear the sound of your voice, but you're not talking, you're pointing! I saw you come out of that store over there and I couldn't think of anything else to say. Do you want to go for coffee?"

I wanted to go with him, but those "girl alarms" were going off. All of the stuff I'd heard about meeting strangers was going through my head. He was this charming, good-looking guy, so I figured he was too good to be true. Besides, I was really self-conscious about my hair, my clothes, and my lack of make-up. I really didn't think I looked so good.

I lied to him and said I wasn't interested in coffee because I just had a late breakfast. He politely asked if I just wanted to go sit and talk somewhere, but I said no to that too. He never stopped smiling at me the whole time. Then he said something like, "Thanks for talking to me. You really made my day. Thanks for your time." Then he just walked away.

As soon as he walked off, I knew I had made a big mistake, but all I could do was watch him walk away. And I mean I watched him walk *all the way away* until I couldn't see him anymore. The whole time I was watching him I kept hoping he'd turn around. I kept trying to get myself to go after him, but I couldn't.

The next week, I was there on the same day at the same time, hoping he would be there too. Maybe he worked there or maybe we had the same day off or something. You know what? I never saw him again.

I don't know anything about that guy. I don't know where he lives or what he does. I can't even tell you his name, but his face is burned into my mind. To this day, I can still see exactly what he looked like and what he was wearing. I remember *everything* about him.

It's been four years now, and it still bothers me. Why didn't I just go for coffee? God, I regret not taking a chance with him. I regret that in a *big* way.

Seize opportunity by the beard,
for it is bald behind.

Bulgarian proverb

There's something about Stephanie
(Ray, medical professional, 44)

Back in high school, I was crazy about a girl named Stephanie. Stephanie was an amazingly beautiful girl. She had long blonde hair and big blue eyes. The rest of her was just as perfect as that pretty face. She made decent money all through school by modeling and doing television commercials.

We spent a lot of time together because we were both in the audio visual club. The AV club! Yeah, we pushed the TV's down the hall on those rolling carts.

What was a girl like her doing in that club, right? That's just it, she was a real person. She was someone who liked you for who you were and not for what clothes you wore or who you hung out with.

She was beautiful, but at the same time you could see her as someone you could talk to. She was very approachable. She had an amazing inner beauty.

I constantly thought about her in a romantic way, but she always had a boyfriend. He was the "alpha male." He was tall, handsome, popular, and athletic. I always figured that with him around, I'd never be anything more than just a friend.

She and I stayed in touch after high school. We met once for breakfast and a few weeks later we took a nice walk along the beach together. During our walk, I told her all about my medical schooling and she told me all about a big television deal she was trying to get with one of the major networks. You can't print the name of the company, but their name is a household word.

As we talked along the beach, I found myself thinking, *This girl you're walking next to is going to be seen all over the world. Guys everywhere are going to know who she is and you're walking with her!* It was really weird.

Like always, I found myself thinking about her in a romantic way, but we had always been just friends. As her friend, there was something about the trust she gave me that I didn't want to betray. If I made a move on her, if I betrayed that trust, she might not have seen me as her friend anymore. She might have thought of me as just another desperate guy, just another loser. Despite my strong feelings, I gave her just a kiss on the cheek when we said goodbye.

About six months later, I got a call from Tina, one of our mutual friends. Tina told me to brace myself for some bad news. She said Stephanie had been in a horrible accident.

It turned out Stephanie *got* that huge television deal. She traveled out west to celebrate, but while attending a party they threw for her, Stephanie and lots of other people were badly injured in an explosion and a terrible fire. There was some problem with the equipment the caterers were using. To Stephanie's credit, most of her burns were due to the fact that she helped other people get out.

Tina told me Stephanie's arms, legs, and face were badly burned. Although she was lucky to be alive, she had sustained second- and third-degree burns over most of her body. All of her hair was burned off too.

By the time I got the phone call, Stephanie had already been in the hospital for weeks. Tina called me because Stephanie, in order to be closer to her family, was being transferred to the hospital in our home town. Tina knew I volunteered at the local hospital and she didn't want me to be shocked or surprised when Stephanie arrived. A day or so after her transfer came through, I made an unannounced visit.

I didn't know what to expect, so I tried to prepare myself for the worst. Despite all of my mental preparations and all of the horrible things I had imagined I would see, it was far worse than I thought. When I came through the doorway, I saw her lying there almost completely unrecognizable. Parts of her body were covered, but other areas which looked badly burned were exposed. Her lips were black, black like charcoal. Her eyelashes were gone and, just as Tina said, all of her long hair had been burned off.

She had the entire hospital room to herself. I was glad to see her treatments had progressed to the point where she wasn't in one of those recovery tents. She didn't know I was there yet, so I took a moment to collect my thoughts. Regardless of how shocked I was, I knew for her sake I had to maintain my composure. I took a deep breath and politely let her know that she had company.

She seemed very happy to see me. I pulled the visitor's chair up close to the edge of her bed and we talked for a long time. It was really awkward at first, but soon we were exchanging small talk and gradually it was as if nothing had happened. It was as if no time at all had passed since we last spoke.

Toward the end of my visit, we began to reminisce. After a few minutes of us talking about the old days, she lifted her arm and swung it out over the edge of the bed. I looked around the room to see if she was gesturing towards or pointing at something, but I couldn't figure out what she wanted. Although her hand was partially bandaged, her ring and pinky finger were unwrapped and she wiggled those two fingers at me. After a second or two, I figured out her little gesture meant, "Please hold my hand."

Up until then, everything said between us was positive and upbeat. Her thin smile and friendly conversation had made it so easy for me to maintain my composure. Now I was afraid that she was going to break down and I wasn't going to be able to be strong for her. As I took her hand, I had to look away because I felt myself start to crumble.

We sat there holding hands in silence for what felt like a very long time. I looked at everything in the room except her. If I looked at her now, I knew I would *not* be able to keep it together. The last thing she needed was for me to get all emotional. I think I ended up looking at the floor a lot.

Several times it seemed as if she started to say something, but she never got past the first syllable. Eventually, with her voice breaking slightly, she said, "I've always wondered why you never asked me out.

I always wanted you to. I wanted us to get to know each other more . . . in that way . . ." Her voice sort of trailed off and I could tell she was trying very hard not to cry.

What she said to me hit me like a punch in the stomach. Whatever worries I had about crying were gone. I smiled and said something pleasant, but I was totally and completely surprised. I never knew that she felt that way about me.

At that moment, it was like the whole world had faded away. It was like my whole life had snuck up on me from behind and knocked me down. I didn't know how to feel.

After I got over the initial shock, I sat there and thought, *Damn, I'm such an ass. All those years, all those wasted opportunities. I've got no guts. No guts at all.*

That little comment of hers couldn't have come at a worse time. I had just gotten serious with someone I had been seeing for a few months and Stephanie still had the same boyfriend as before. Besides that, her horrible injuries guaranteed that her life would be far from normal for a very long time. You know that expression, "A day late and a dollar short"? Well, that was me.

Looking back, I don't think she told me those things for any particular reason. It wasn't like she expected us to begin a relationship right then and there. She was struggling with this terrible life-changing event and she must have been feeling very vulnerable. I guess it caused her to look at herself and reevaluate some of the choices she had made, that's all.

Sometimes I wish she hadn't told me those things. It's kind of rough to carry that around now. I *cannot believe* how stupid I was. I'll tell you one thing though: after that, I had a lot more guts with women, *a lot* more.

Ray and I talked for quite a while after he told me Stephanie's story. We covered all of my usual interview questions, but no matter what else we talked about, my mind kept wandering back to her. If it wasn't for the fact that I'd known Ray for nearly 15 years and he was an extremely well-respected member of the local medical community, I'm not sure I would have believed him. After all, even if I tried, I don't think I could have made up a story as powerful and symbolic as that one.

For a long time, I considered this story to be a lesson Ray had learned. I viewed it as a hard lesson in regret; the price paid for romantic cowardice. All of that is still true, but I now see there's so much more to the story. It's really Stephanie's story.

Instead of seeing this through Ray's eyes, try to see it through Stephanie's. Imagine for a moment that you were Stephanie. Try to see yourself lying in that hospital bed.

Although you were clearly not one of those stereotypical unattainable popular girls (and all of the negative connotations that come with those labels), much of your life and life experiences revolved around your appearance. The modeling jobs you had, the attention you received, all of those things were because of your beauty. Perhaps even the friends and boyfriend you had were yours for the same reason. We are all judged by the way we look, but perhaps you were judged a bit more than the rest of us.

And as you lay there in that bed, did your mind play tricks on you? Did you wonder if the world as you knew it would slip away? Did your friends like you for who you were or for what you looked like? Would they still be your friends? Did you wonder if your handsome and popular boy friend would still be there for you?

Just then, Ray walked into your hospital room. Ray liked you. You were neither his trophy girlfriend nor one of his sexual conquests. You weren't even someone about whom he could brag to his friends, but he liked you just the same. Yes, he was attracted to you, but he always thought of you as more than just a pretty face. He liked you for who you were.

And as you lay there with much of your body badly burned, he was there for you. As best he could, he tried to be strong for you. When you held his hand, you saw him nervously avert his gaze. You saw his jaw clench as he fought off tears. You always saw something special in him and that day was no exception.

And as you lay there wondering if everyone else in your world—your friends, your handsome boyfriend, and your television network "friends" —would still care, maybe you wished you had not waited until now to hold his hand. Maybe you wished that back in high school you had held out your hand and wiggled those two fingers at that boy in the AV club.

Although I have never met Stephanie, I think about her almost every day.

*It is not only for what we do
that we are held responsible,
but also for what we do not do.*

Molière (1622–1673)
French playwright

Careers

*Whenever it is in any way possible, every boy
and girl should choose as their life work some
occupation which they should like to do anyhow,
even if they did not need the money.*

William Lyon Phelps (1865–1943)
American journalist, essayist, and Yale professor

Ten feet tall and bulletproof

My father always told my brother and me to choose a career in a field we liked. "Do what you love," he would always say.

My dad had a very stressful but successful career as an insurance agent. It was not something he enjoyed, but it was very lucrative. He worked long hours, six days a week, for over 20 years in order to build up his business. He kept up that pace until he had a heart attack at the age of 46.

This valuable lesson was not lost on me. Regardless of what I chose to do in life, I knew it would have to be something I enjoyed doing. I promised myself I would do something I loved.

After graduating from college, I did not make good on that promise. Because I had absolutely no idea what to do, I went to work at my father's office. I worked there for a while, but like my father, I did not enjoy it very much. If I stayed in that career I knew I would not be happy.

All during this time I was learning to fly gliders. A few years earlier when I had made my life list, I had put "Learn to fly" near the top. It was during my last semester of college that I began to take lessons. It became a real obsession of mine.

Despite all of my passion for aviation, it simply never occurred to me that I might be able to become a professional pilot. Subconsciously

I thought, *Well, you've got to be an ex-military pilot to do that. You've got to be ten feet tall and bulletproof to get those jobs.* In truth, I never asked anyone about it because I figured I had just as much chance of becoming an airline pilot as I had of becoming an astronaut.

As luck would have it, I ran into an old high school friend at the doctor's office one day. After we exchanged pleasantries, he told me that he was leaving the next day to attend a flight school in Florida. He told me that his goal was to become an airline pilot.

Because I was a bit confused, I asked him how that was possible. He was a civilian, he wore glasses, and he had already finished college. (The only flight schools for civilians I had ever heard about were regular four-year colleges.) What sort of a school trains people like us to become professional pilots? His answers proved to be quite an education for me. Two months later, I joined him at the same Florida flight academy.

Before I left for flight school, I drove out to the airport to say goodbye to the guys in my glider club. When I got there, I found the usual characters hanging out in one of the messy little Quonset huts that made up the once active but now dusty old Air Force base. My former instructor was supportive, but it was easy to see he didn't think I had *any* chance of getting hired by the major airlines. He said, "Jimmy, are you *sure* they hire guys like us?" Not knowing the answer, I smiled, shook his hand, and headed off to find out.

The next ten years of my life were spent in search of an answer to my glider instructor's question. After an amazing year in flight school, I spent the next eight years working in several low-paying but very difficult and demanding flying jobs. The first of these jobs was a two-year stint working as a flight instructor for $9,800 a year.

My "big" break came in the winter of 1992 when I got hired by a commuter airline. My annual income skyrocketed to $17,000. For four and a half long years, I flew in and out of New England, eastern Canada, and all of the cities in the northeastern United States. Without an autopilot or a decent weather radar unit, I bounced around in a 19-seat turbo prop aircraft, paying my dues and gaining valuable experience.

In the summer of 1996, after going through a rigorous interview process, I got hired at TWA. My salary soared to $24,000 a year.

Despite the fact that my co-workers were second to none, I stayed with TWA for only 18 months. The handwriting on the wall was unmistakable; the company would not last. Roughly four years before TWA made its final flight, I managed to get out.

December of 1997, I got hired at one of the largest airlines in the world. The flaming hoops I jumped through to get the job are too numerous to mention. All I'll say is it was worth the effort. The last year of my ten-year journey was spent completing their training program and going through their mandatory 12-month probationary period. After that, I had finally arrived.

The day my probation ended, I remember walking proudly through the crowded airport and catching a glimpse of my reflection in one of the huge terminal windows. Standing there in my uniform, it was the first time I realized it had been ten years since I shook my glider instructor's hand and headed off to flight school. *Ten years.*

Roughly a year ago, I ran into my old glider instructor while shopping in one of those big home supply stores. It had been nearly 15 years since we had last seen each other, and he didn't recognize me at first. After a moment or two, he raised his eyebrows and a big smile came across his face. He introduced me to his fiancé and she stood there and smiled politely while we told a few of our old stories.

Eventually, we got around to talking about what we were doing now. He said that he had retired and was enjoying his newfound freedom. When I told him I was flying a B737-800 for one of the biggest airlines in the world, a look of amazement came over him. Not saying a word, he slowly shifted his eyes from me to his fiancé and back again. Slowly, he extended his hand to me and broke the silence by saying,

"*My* Jimmy? *My* Jimmy flies those big jets? Well, I'll be damned!" He shook my hand hard and we laughed.

We stood and talked for a while, but my old instructor's face never quite recovered from the shock. Finally, we shook hands again, said our goodbyes, and went our separate ways. As I walked away, I looked over my shoulder and saw him doing the same: smiling at me over his shoulder.

Perhaps I'm wrong, but I'd like to think his surprise was due to his assumptions about the world rather than his opinion of my skill as a pilot. I'd like to think he was shocked to discover that the assumptions he made all those years ago were wrong. In the end, the airlines did hire "guys like us" and it amazed him.

My former instructor was not marveling at me or anything about me. He was just getting a glimpse of another reality, another world filled with different choices. Most likely, a world he never even knew was there. A world I went looking for, and thankfully, I found.

It was about this very thing that I asked those I interviewed. What were some of the things they went looking for? Did they look for any particular job or career, or did they just stumble upon whatever it is they're now doing? Whether they went looking or not, were they happy with what they found? What, if anything, would they do differently?

Going to the chapel
(Darlene, wedding planner, 29)

I got out of college with a degree in International Hotel Management. The hotel job I got after graduation was awful. It didn't interest me at all. I stuck with it for as long as I did because I needed the money and I was unsure of what else to do.

The only part of the job that I liked was the event planning I got to do. All hotels have conventions, weddings, reunions, etc. These things need to be organized and arranged properly. I enjoyed that. I *really* enjoyed planning the handful of weddings that we got every year.

I used to talk to my husband constantly about starting my own business as a wedding planner, but that's all I did: talk. He kept asking me why I wasn't doing anything about it and I always had some excuse. This went on for a few years.

My husband knew how much I loved talking about it, so he used to get me going by asking me things like, "So, what will your company name be?" One day, he even asked me for a couple of backup names, just in case my favorite one was already taken. Thinking nothing of it, I told him a few of my ideas and went off to work.

When I got home later that night he said, "Your company is up and running!" He had gone on the Internet and formed a corporation in my name. He was also able to use my favorite company name—my *first* choice for my business as a wedding planner. I was *so* excited.

My husband showed me the Internet site he used to set it all up and there it was, my name, my company name, all of it. It was such a thrill to see it in print. That excitement was magnified ten times when all of the company paperwork arrived at our house.

Because of my husband's support, I felt able to go forward. Within a few weeks of seeing my company name on that computer screen, I quit my job at the hotel. There's been no turning back ever since.

I can't tell you how glad I am that he gave me that first push. Setting me up like that was incredible. Incorporating my business wasn't everything, but it got me going. If he hadn't done that, I would still be just talking about doing it.

My husband and I don't have a lot of money right now, but it's not necessary for me to make big money in order to feel successful. It's more important for me to enjoy what I do. My new job, or maybe I should call it my new career, uses my hobbies and my interests. *That* makes it great. I do enjoy it very much and because of that, I consider myself successful.

I still get nervous when I see how much money goes out versus how much comes in, but I feel confident things will be all right. I've never had any doubts about my abilities. On occasion, I *have* had doubts about how to get new clients. All I can do is to do my best.

Do I regret not doing this sooner? I'm not sure. Maybe, but maybe I wasn't ready then; I don't know. All I know for sure is that this is me. This is my life now.

Whatever you can do or dream you can, begin it.
Boldness has genius, power, and magic in it.

Johan Wolfgang von Goethe (1749–1832)
German playwright and philosopher

 # Who I am
(Suzy, educator/former corporate executive, 41)

Up until recently, I never really chose a career; my parents chose one for me. Ever since I can remember, they always told me what to do. Sadly, I always listened.

Back in school, my ideas about careers revolved around creativity and working with other people. One of my earliest desires was to become a writer. When my parents heard that they said, "That's a starving profession." They pushed me towards what they felt was a more lucrative career. Off I went to business school.

Immediately, I knew it wasn't for me. Most of the areas of study were very technical. I found it to be way too dry.

I didn't seem to fit in with my classmates either. They all seemed like a cut-throat gang, ready to take on the wild world of business. I was just a kid from the suburbs.

By focusing on the management training courses they offered, I found a way to fit in. Those classes were about dealing with and training other people. That allowed me to work with real human beings and not numbers. It allowed me to be true to myself *and* to my parent's wishes. For a while, it seemed to work out.

After graduation, I entered the business world and did the best I could. Over the next 15 years, there were good times and bad times. When I was single, the money and the promotions kept me going, but that got old quickly. The 70-hour workweeks, the phone calls in the middle of the night, the beeper going off on my days off, it never ended. I stayed with it for as long as I did simply because I knew nothing else. It was my life.

Ironically, it was a motivational seminar sponsored by *my* company that finally pushed me to quit. During the course of their three-day seminar, they gave us several tests that focused on revealing our personalities, our motivations, and our goals. *What an eye opener.*

I decided to answer the test questions honestly rather than the way I thought a person in my position should answer them. The types of questions weren't yes/no or multiple choice, they were all supposed to be things to reflect on. Some of the questions were: *Where do you see yourself in five years? If a perfect stranger followed you around for 24 hours, would they know what was important to you based on the things you said and did? Are you living your life true to your priorities and values?*

There were other interesting questions, but no matter what they asked, my honest answers told me my career was a lie. I was *not* living true to my priorities and values. Although I had always felt uncomfortable at work, seeing my answers to those questions was the last straw. I finally realized I didn't want to give them my life anymore. I decided to quit.

In all of my previous jobs, I always loved anything to do with teaching or training. Those were the only parts of my work that ever made me feel fulfilled. Because of that realization, I began looking into becoming a teacher.

When I interviewed for my current teaching job, they said, "We can't offer you the type of money you're used to." I said, "That's okay. That's not my top priority anymore." That was the truth; it wasn't. I told them all I needed was to feel like I was helping people. Two weeks later, I had the job.

With my fiancé's help, I've come to see a new path for myself. For the first time, I can honestly say I'm doing what I love. You can't believe what a difference it makes in your life.

Now that the crazy world of business is behind me, I say to myself, "God, what was I thinking back then?" Now when we're out on the boat, my fiancé teases me by saying, "Hey, where's your beeper?" Sometimes we listen to the traffic report in the morning and laugh. I don't miss it at all. Not even a little.

A musician must make music, an artist must paint,
a poet must write, if he is to be ultimately at peace
with himself. What a man can be, he must be.

Abraham Harold Maslow (1908–1970)
American psychologist, developer of the
"hierarchy of needs/self-actualization" theory

 # Your own totem pole
(Roberta, marketing assistant, 63)

I'm not in a rewarding job now. A few years ago, I was working for another company as the personal assistant to one of their vice presidents. *That* was a great job. My boss was a rising star at that company, and I rose right along with him. We were on top back then, but in the business world, things happen.

The company was bought out by people who didn't like the VP

I worked for. They ended up getting rid of both of us. It didn't matter to them how well I did *my* job; our fates were locked together. They just kept demoting him, and me, until we were out the door.

That whole thing made me realize the importance of independence and having your own identity in business. In that world, you gain independence not by being an Indian, but by being a Chief. If you own your own totem pole, that's even better.

Coming down after having a great job was pretty tough. I got another job right away, but I was in my late fifties then. Starting over at that age was not good. I'm 63 now and I feel like I *have* to keep working. I've got no real benefits. I've got no pension. It's a different world out there, let me tell you.

If I could do it over again, I'd be something like a counselor for teenage girls, or better yet, an interior decorator. People are always telling me I have a real flair for decorating. That's what I should be doing right now.

About seven years ago, a friend got behind me and pushed me towards starting my own decorating business. She sat me down at breakfast one day and said, "Come on Bertie, you're smart; you've got the eye for it. You owe it to yourself to give it a try."

I thought about it, but the bottom line was I was too afraid. All I could see was the downside, the embarrassment of failure. I was even afraid my prospective clients would ask me if I had a degree in interior design, which I did not. I was too scared to do it, so I didn't. I really regret that.

In this life, you've got to take your strengths and go with them. Whatever your dream is, you've got to chase it. It doesn't matter if you're new at it or even if you're scared of doing it—you'll think of something.

Ten months after this interview, I contacted Roberta in order to get a few story details that I missed during our first meeting. To my surprise, she told me that upon returning to work from a recent vacation, she was met at the front door of her office building by corporate security personnel. She was escorted to the human resources department where she was told that, along with 42 of her co-workers, she was being laid off. She was escorted to her desk, given ten minutes to collect her things, and she was then escorted out of the building.

Fortune favors the brave.

Virgil (70–19 B.C.)
Roman playwright

 # Eyes open
(Jeff, computer technician, 43)

Since I was 11 years old, whenever I had a day off, my father took me to work with him. My dad was a plumber and he'd take me out in his truck wherever he went. We'd be gone from 6:30 in the morning until 6:30 at night. I knew what it was to work.

My first real job was working at a government laboratory. Because of my work ethic, I made myself available to my bosses seven days a week. I was always on call or coming in on my days off, but I didn't really mind. The way I looked at it, it was my job, it was my responsibility. In fact, I often got angry at my co-workers for not shouldering their share of the load. There were a lot of "government job slackers" working at that place.

For 13 years, my annual reviews were always perfect. I was a model employee. Something that happened during my last annual review turned out to be a major turning point in my career.

In my thirteenth year with the lab, I decided to take a computer networking class at night. My boss and my supervisors all knew about the class. In fact, they thought it was a great idea. They encouraged me to do it. That's why the rest of this story is so ridiculous.

Part of what I did at the lab was to keep the particle accelerator up and running. One day, the thing broke down. Two co-workers and I spent hours working on the problem. Instead of leaving at 4:30 P.M., which was my usual quitting time, I stayed three extra hours to try to fix what was broken. No one asked me to stay. I felt it was my responsibility.

My supervisor knew about my class. He also knew it was the last class of the semester and the final was going to be given that night. When 7:30 P.M. rolled around, he said, "Go. There are two of us here. We've got it. Go ahead." So I left.

Weeks later, when it came time for my annual review, I figured it would be the same as all of the others. I walked into it without any doubt about what they would say. After all, I was still a great employee and an asset to the lab.

As soon as my review began, I noticed the members of the review board were acting a bit hostile towards me. My manager finally got to the point: He said when I had left to go to my class that night, I had walked out on my job. He said I had been derelict in my duties.

It was like a scene out of a movie. You know how it is when someone in the movies gets bad news, the background blurs, and the camera zooms in to show the look of shock on their face? Well, that's how I felt.

That place was my life. I worked like a *dog* for them. They picked at me and criticized me for missing *one night*. Thirteen years of dedication and they chose *one night* to focus on. Within two weeks, I had a new job.

Since I left the lab, my career has really taken off. In addition to having a better paying job, I now have the confidence to pursue other business interests on the side. For several years now, I have been responsible for the creation and the management of a website for a small newspaper. Instead of working like a dog for someone else, I'm now doing it for myself.

There's a friend of mine who's still working at the lab. I call him every once in a while. He complains about working hard and not being appreciated, but he does nothing about it. Whenever I tell him he should go out on his own and try something else, he always tells me why he can't. He tells me about his bills and his money problems. I tell him we *all* have bills and problems. He just doesn't want to hear it.

Every time I speak to my old co-worker, I learn something. Those conversations remind me of who I once was and they also push me towards the person who I still want to become. I'm glad I got started.

In hindsight, the disrespect my old managers showed me during my annual review was one of the best things that ever happened to me. It woke me up to the fact that I had been in a rut for so many years. It made me realize I was wasting my talent in a place where I was not appreciated.

> *Work while you have the light. You are responsible*
> *for the talent that has been entrusted to you.*
>
> Henri-Frédéric Amiel (1821–1881)
> Swiss philosopher

 ## Nine years and eleven months
(Rick, partner and branch manager of a brokerage house, 41)

You can't hit a target you don't see. That kind of sums up what my life was like through high school and college. I had no direction.

People would ask me, "What do you want to do?" but I didn't know. I ended up as a biology major in college. I figured I'd be *something*.

So I went through four years of college, and they went quickly, but I still didn't have any direction. My focus was just to get *out* of school, nothing else. I just wanted to fill in that square.

To help pay for school, I started working at a facility for adults who were profoundly retarded. It became a pretty comfortable job. I went to work and did crossword puzzles all night. After I graduated, I stayed on and ended up becoming the night supervisor.

I wasn't going anywhere and I *knew* I wasn't going anywhere, but I didn't mind. Maybe I was in denial about the whole thing. Maybe I didn't want to think about where it was going to lead or what my next step should be.

For a single guy, I was making decent money. It was enough to pay my rent and buy me a car, so that's where I stayed for nine years and eleven months: living day to day. Complacency is a *real* killer.

One night, this guy I worked with told me how much his friend was making as a stockbroker. *That* conversation was interesting. I didn't know anything about stockbrokers or what you had to do to become one. I figured you had to know somebody or have a degree in it or something. It turned out that none of the things I thought were true. All you had to do was pass a written test called "the series seven" and that was it, you were a stockbroker. I told that guy he had to ask his friend to get us jobs wherever he worked.

Now I had a target; I was going to *be* something. I was going to become a stockbroker. I knew what I had to do to get there and I began doing it.

I quit my job and lived off of my small savings while I studied for the test. I studied nine hours a day for a month and a half. Once I passed, I got hired by a big firm and started taking their sales training course.

The first firm I worked for wasn't perfect, but they had an *amazing* training program. Everybody would meet three times a day. One of those meetings was just a "rah-rah" type of thing, but the other two were really good. Guys would tell little stories or anecdotes about the business, successful sales they made, making money, whatever. There were lots of visits from motivational speakers, too.

They knew that we never learned about motivation or goals in school. They taught us that success and goal-setting was a process. We just followed the steps.

Our instructors used the purchase of a house as an example. They said, "If you want to buy a house and can't afford it, the purchase price might seem completely out of reach. First, decide how much of a down payment you will need and work backwards from there. How much would you have to earn in commissions to get that much money? Figure out how many sales you would need to make in order to earn that much in commissions. How many clients would you have to meet with in order to generate that many sales? Figure out how many cold calls you'd need to make in order to set up that many client meetings. It's a simple numbers game." And they were right.

The one idea that they put above everything else was the importance of affirmations. Affirmations are beliefs. The idea is to make yourself believe in the things you want, the things you want to come true.

They told us to write our affirmations down and put them where we'd see them. We put them on our desks, on our refrigerators, in our cars, everywhere.

A few of my affirmations were:

- I am successful.
- I open new accounts at will.
- I'm the hardest working person I know.
- I make one less mistake every day.

The best thing about affirmations is they don't have to be true—they *become* true. They used to say to us, "If you repeat it to yourself long enough, then the lie becomes the truth." The idea is to begin to convince yourself that you can succeed. It worked. I *did* succeed.

The guys who ran the training department used a made-up word that perfectly describes my old life. They said, "It's easy to be comfortable. What's *not* easy is stepping out of your *comfortability* zone."

You know, it *was* comfortable for me to sit on a couch and watch over profoundly retarded adults all night. It was a living, but I wasn't going anywhere with it. At some point, you know, I had to quit that job and take a chance.

That was about eight years ago. Now I'm a partner and a branch manager for a nationally known brokerage firm. I own my own home, I've got a great car, and my finances are solid. In an average month, I make four times as much as I did at my old job. Nothing about me has changed; I'm still the same person. The difference is I finally had a target to go after.

> *Plan for the future, because that is where*
> *you are going to spend the rest of your life.*

> Mark Twain (1835–1910)
> American writer, humorist, and lecturer

# The natural choice
(Mary, retired elementary school teacher, 62)

Fortunately, I picked a great career for myself. I've always seen myself as an educator. It really is who I am. My career has *always* been my identity.

I've always loved children, even when I was little. My mother always said that even as a toddler, I'd run over to everyone's stroller or baby carriage to see the baby inside. The love I have for kids is incredible.

The most rewarding thing about my job was getting to see real results. There was a direct relationship between my skills as a teacher and the skills and development of my students. My success equaled their success and vice versa. Every September, a new class of frightened little children would file into my classroom. In June, they would leave as confident little kids. Where else can you see those sorts of results?

Teaching a child to read is an amazing thing. When you see the little light bulb come on over their head, it's an indescribable feeling. *That's* phenomenal.

In addition to the satisfaction I got from it, there was an incredible emotional value, too. The love I got from those kids was amazing! They gave me so much more than I ever gave them.

They'd always come up to me and tell me that they loved me. On parent/teacher conference nights, the parents would sometimes share special things the kids had said about me. It made me feel so happy. Half the time, I didn't know whether to laugh or cry.

Oh, the gifts! The gifts the kids gave me were so sweet they melted my heart. It didn't matter what the gifts were, they were all special. In my last year teaching, one of my kids gave me a used lipstick for Christmas. *That* was adorable. Everything was wonderful. It was all wonderful.

One year, a girl gave me a bag of cherry tomatoes. I remember thinking it was a very unusual gift to receive from a seven-year-old girl. I was glad to have them because I was hungry.

When I took the tomatoes to the teachers' lounge and began eating them, I saw another teacher giving me funny looks. It turned out the tomatoes belonged to her. My student had stolen them from her and given them to me! My student was suspended and I ended up having to home school her. Okay, *that* wasn't so wonderful.

I was blessed to have found something rewarding to do with my life. The idea is to choose something you can be passionate about. If you can do that, then your job becomes a part of you. If you can do *that*, you'll never really have a job.

Political science
(Chris, engineer/project developer, 40)

School does not give you the skill set to survive, let alone succeed, in the business world. School teaches you that all you have to do is have the right answers on the test to do well. It came as a shock to me to find out that even though my academic background had prepared me for the technical aspects of my job, I was *completely* unprepared for the people skills required.

In the field of engineering, things are black and white. Things are either right or they're wrong. That's how things were presented in school and that's how I understood things to be. As long as I added up the numbers and had the right answer, I'd always be right. When I took that attitude of mine out into the business world, I got squashed.

For example, two years ago, I was working for a female supervisor. I never got along with her, but I didn't see it as a real problem. No matter what her agenda was, I always had the data. I always had my research in order.

After all, facts are facts. If I knew I was right, then by default, she had to be wrong. It was in one of those moments of certainty that I contradicted her in a meeting. As you might guess, our business relationship got a lot worse after that.

All of the employees where I work receive performance ratings at the end of each year. They range from 1 to 5, with 1 being the best, and 5 being the worst. The same year that I had that problem with my supervisor, I was the *number one* producer in my department. I was personally responsible for bringing in over 1.5 million dollars. My numbers were so good that the second best performer in my department was over a million dollars behind me.

With that in mind, what would you have expected my performance rating to be? I was expecting it to be a 1, *maybe* a 2. *It was a 4.*

To say I was shocked was an understatement. Weren't we trying to run a business here? In a business, don't the numbers matter? Don't they always talk about "the bottom line"? *I* was the top producer for the department. *I* had the data. *I* had the facts.

It was then I realized how naive I was. The company I worked for wasn't just a business, it was a group of people. It didn't matter that it was a global company with tens of thousands of employees; it was *still* all about dealing with other people.

I had been technically correct throughout my entire career as an engineer, but that conflict with my supervisor taught me that coming to the end of the equation with the correct answer was not the only thing to consider. I learned that dealing with other people correctly is more important than *being* correct.

The very next year, I didn't perform nearly as well in terms of dollars, but I received a much higher performance rating. The *only* reason why that happened was because I made it a point to work on my people skills. I didn't have to change my behavior that much. Just a few small changes made all of the difference. All I did was become a little more open, a little more flexible. I stopped challenging my supervisor's decisions and I never contradicted her again.

Believe it or not, the idea of "going along to get along" can take you a lot farther than just your education. Your education gets you invited to the party, but it's your social skills that determine whether or not you get to stay.

Windows that open and close
(Larry, police officer/small business owner, 41)

Never go anywhere because of a boss; never stay anywhere because of a boss. Bosses come and go. If you change your career plans because of some manager or supervisor, you're cheating yourself out of a lot of opportunities.

In the Police Department, your chance to transfer can be brief. Staffing and manpower levels are always changing. At any given time, some doors are open and other doors are closed. You have to be ready to make your move when the opportunity arises.

For several years, there were job openings in our Special Enforcement unit. I had always wanted to transfer there, but I never did. The thing that kept me from doing it was I hated the Special Enforcement unit boss. I couldn't stand him.

As with all of those transfers, the window of opportunity stayed open for a while, but then it closed. To add insult to injury, shortly after the window closed, the boss I hated came over to where *I* work. Now he's here and my chance to get into the other unit is gone. It doesn't get any dumber than that.

People knowledge
(Darren, attorney, 36)

I live in an expensive area of the country. Now that I'm a newlywed and my wife and I are looking to buy a house, I can't afford one. Here I am, this smart, hard-working attorney, but I can't even buy a house in the area where I grew up. I realize now I've been working hard for my boss all these years, whereas I *should* have been working hard for myself.

Everything I did to prepare for a law career made sense until I went looking for my first job. The vast majority of the people with whom I graduated from law school took jobs in the city. With all of the crime and the strange people, there was *no way* I was going to take part in that. The city always intimidated me and I never even *thought* to work there. Instead, I took a job in the suburbs. That turned out to be a pretty big career mistake.

It wasn't until several years later that I realized the city jobs carried the money; the city jobs had the prestige. You might be wondering why I didn't know about the important differences between city jobs and suburban jobs back when I could have done something about it. Well, that's been my problem for as long as I can remember. I've always been naive. At crucial points in my life, no one clued me into things. At any given moment along the way, I never knew what I should have known.

An embarrassing example of what I'm talking about took place when I was a junior in high school. I found out about the junior prom two days before prom night. I was so out of it, I didn't even know there *was* a junior prom. That sort of naiveté has stayed with me over the years.

Every law school has a very prestigious organization called The Law Review. To join, you have to have good grades *and* you have to submit a sample of your writing. I only found out about The Law Review *after* the submission deadline had passed. No one could believe that I had been so oblivious to the deadline. The truth, which I was too embarrassed to tell anyone, was I had never even *heard* of The Law Review.

It's not something I can easily explain, but things like that used to happen to me all the time. They still do. They happen because I've led such a cloistered life. I've never known about a lot of things because I don't interact with other people that much. It's from talking to other people that you learn about the world.

I've always seen myself as being sort of like the absent-minded professor. I've always had a lot of book knowledge. My SAT scores were great, my IQ was high enough to get me into Mensa, but I lack what I call "people knowledge." That's really what's held me back.

People knowledge can be defined as the ability to talk with others and to identify with them. Someone with a good knowledge of people knows how to start conversations, to make others feel at ease, and to get others to like them. When it comes down to it, if it's a choice

between book knowledge and people knowledge, it's people knowledge that will lead to success.

The things I'm talking about are sometimes called "EQ" or "emotional quotient." A few things that fall under the heading of EQ are self-regard, assertiveness, and independence. These are definitely my weakest areas. I've always been too timid, played it too safe. After so many years of being this way, it's almost impossible to change.

It's hard to accept the fact that I'm not nearly as successful as a lot of the stupid people I meet. The idea that it's confident and outgoing people who succeed *does* make sense to me. It makes sense in theory, but it's pretty tough to stomach it in reality.

On some level, I still think that being smart should count for something. When it comes to my job, nobody is more diligent than me. No one works harder than me. So where did things go wrong?

My parents, like all of my teachers in school, always said things like, "You're really smart. You'll definitely be a success." I sort of took it for granted that I would walk right into things. With that mindset, I coasted through school and through my career with blinders on. I assumed that the world would come to *me*. Nine years into this career of mine, I now see that the world doesn't come to anyone. In fact, it seems to have passed me by.

With regard to my career, I'm playing it safe, just like I always have, but I'm paying the price for it too. Like a few of my friends, I could go out on my own and start my own practice, but I can't seem to do it. There are too many irrational fears holding me back. Too many years of sitting around waiting for the world to come to me, I guess.

I'm not going to blame anybody. I know life isn't fair. It's just that I'd trade away some of these IQ points of mine for some confidence, an outgoing personality, or a more motivated spirit.

Man stands in his own shadow and wonders why it is dark.

Zen saying

85

The echo effect

The most interesting and unexpected thing that happened while writing this book was discovering how the process itself had affected some of the people I interviewed. Whether they did not like the stories they ended up telling me and decided to make changes in their lives, whether they found themselves haunted *again* by the same mistakes they shared during their interviews, or whether they found the idea behind the book compelling enough to begin to live differently, several of them had their own words and experiences bounce back at them shortly after we spoke.

Those I interviewed who experienced this "echo effect" took it upon themselves to contact me and share their new stories. They managed to do this even though, for some of them, there was no easy way to reach me. Their determination to share their new experiences fueled my passion for this project.

Doug, the interviewee who told me that wonderful story about his epiphany on the streets of Florence, was one of the members of the echo effect club. What you don't know about Doug is that he's one of a handful of people who were at the center of the airborne chaos on September 11, 2001. No one alive today who was flying an airplane that morning was closer to what happened than Doug. The only ones who saw more and knew more are no longer with us.

His story is an amazing one which is unfortunately too long and complicated to be included in this book. His airborne ordeal lasted for hours. All the while, the FAA, the Air Force, the FBI, and Doug himself were convinced his flight had been scheduled for a takeover by the terrorists. At the very least, they thought there was a bomb on the flight.

For hours, Doug flew on, thinking at any minute someone might come through the cockpit door and kill him. During their excruciatingly slow final descent, he thought their plane would be destroyed by a barometrically sensitive bomb thought to be onboard. When he finally landed, his plane was stormed by FBI agents, guns drawn.

For months after the incident, Doug tried to maintain his position as a pilot, but his worsening post-traumatic stress disorder symptoms eventually forced him out of the career he loved. He has spent roughly the last two years working on developing and marketing a software program of his own design, but it's been a struggle.

It had been almost a year since our interview, but after experiencing the echo effect one day during a meeting, he picked up the phone and called me long distance from California to tell me this story.

The gift
(Doug, entrepreneur/former airline pilot, 40)

Two days ago, I had a meeting with a disability attorney. I needed to see him to find out if I had any rights that needed protecting, or if I had any financial options at all. Apparently, you can get some money from the government if you're disabled.

Right off the bat, the attorney seemed like a good guy. He was about my height, gray hair, in his mid-sixties. His little office was cluttered with stacks of papers and all kinds of books. Lots of paperback books, stuff about exploration and personal development. You can tell a lot about somebody by their books. I could tell this guy wasn't one of those tweedy lawyers; he was more of a California type.

Anyway, it was a weirdly powerful meeting. This was supposed to be some cold and impersonal get-together, but we sat there and talked for about 30 minutes. We really connected.

I told the guy my 9/11 story and he was completely blown away. He was apologetic about the reality of my situation, and he also let me know that he empathized with me. He told me about a car accident that he was in 11 years before and how it really put things in perspective for him. *He actually got choked up.*

As nice as the guy was, the real reason I went was to find out if I was eligible for any government disability money. Well, no dice. He said I wasn't entitled to anything.

Usually, I'm a "glass half full" kind of a guy, but the news the attorney gave me really brought me down. You know, the entrepreneurial thing hasn't hit yet, I'm running out of money, I turned 40 just a month ago, and I feel like I'm running out of time.

Lately, I've been looking at myself and wondering, *What the hell happened to me?* I used to have a job. I used to have a future. What gives? Hell, I walked *into* the meeting feeling sorry for myself.

Eventually, the meeting wound down and it was time for me to go. As he walked me out, I could tell he wanted to say something, but he kept changing his mind. He'd turn to look at me, take a breath in through his mouth, but then he'd look away towards the door.

When we got out in the hallway by the elevator, he put his hand on my shoulder and said, "Look, it isn't my place to preach, but I would tell you this is a gift." I gave him a funny look and said something dismissive like, "Oh, it's a *gift* huh?" What I was thinking was, *I am screwed and this guy isn't getting it.*

You have to understand, platitudes are a pet peeve of mine. They drive me *insane.* They're the types of things that people say when they have no idea what else to say. I *hate* it when people give me that "everything happens for a reason" crap. I never even liked hearing it said to anyone else, but now *I'd* been listening to it nonstop for over two years.

He picked up on my sarcasm, but it didn't stop him. He got really serious and said, "Really. This thing is a gift." I think I said, "Well, that's a gift you can keep." The elevator doors opened and I stepped in, but he didn't want to let it go. He followed me into the elevator.

I began to feel a little bad about blowing him off. He had been really nice to me and I figured he deserved a bit more than my cynicism, so I turned towards him and saw he was looking at the floor of the elevator like he was working out a math problem. Then he looked up at me and said, "When men get into their 40s, they look back and wonder why they let a 21-year-old kid decide the course of their lives. It's a time when a lot of guys go through divorces and changes. This is an amazing opportunity for you. You can do *anything* now."

When we got down to the lobby, I shook his hand and thanked him for what he said. He wished me luck and got back on the elevator. That was it.

You know how it is when you hear something that's true, but you really don't want to hear it? That's what it felt like. I was annoyed, but as I walked out to my car, I couldn't stop thinking about it.

One of the first things that went through my mind was the premise of *your* book. Here was this guy, this 65-year-old guy reaching out and telling me I had the chance to choose my future. It was almost like I was coming back to talk to myself, an older version of me talking to a younger version, setting myself straight.

The thing that happened to me in Florence was all about the stuff from my past that I *can't* fix. I can't go back and straighten out my 17-year-old self, but what that attorney said to me was sort of the opposite of what I felt in Florence. As an older guy, he was reaching back and trying to set *me* straight. It was about something I *could* change; something still ahead of me.

Sometimes you have the ability to step outside the moment and see things you can't see when you're in the moment. As I drove home, I had one of those moments of clarity. It all happened so quickly, the meeting with that guy, hearing what he said, but it was really powerful. It was really weird.

By the time I pulled into my driveway, I had this strange and comforting feeling that everything was going to be all right.

A moment's insight is sometimes worth a life's experience.

Oliver Wendell Holmes (1809–1894)
American poet and essayist

The river visual

When I'm at work, one of my favorite things to do is to fly the river visual approach into Washington National Airport. Most of the pilots with whom I work enjoy it too because you twist and turn and slowly descend as you follow the river southeast to the airport. I enjoy the approach for the same reasons, but for me, that's not what makes it special.

There's a park right at the northern end of the airport. It has a playing field and some jogging and bicycle paths that wind their way off to the west. As long as there's daylight and the weather is good, a small crowd of people gathers there every day.

Because we pass less than 300 feet above the park on our descent, I can always see these people clearly. They do not have jogging clothes or sports uniforms on. They do not have bicycles with them nor do they seem to be there to participate in any other activity.

They all stand there and face us as we descend towards them. As we get closer, they all do the same thing: they raise their hands to their face and they shield their eyes from the sun. They watch us as we get closer and closer until they have to twist around as we pass overhead.

It would be safe to assume that all of these people have jobs, friends, families, and hobbies. Like most of us, I'm sure they value their free time and have no desire to squander what little of it they have doing something foolish. Whether it is their day off, their lunch hour, or one of their sick days, these people gather there to watch us. They gather there every day to watch people like me do what I do for a living. I love seeing them there because, every day, their presence tells me that I have made the right choice. Seeing them reminds me of what my father used to say: "Do what you love."

Those people in the park in Washington D.C. do not gather there because they think I am anything special. They are not there to see me. They are there to see something else: another life, another place, another choice. They stand there to get a glimpse of something outside of their own experience. Perhaps they're there to see a life or a path they wanted for themselves, but did not choose.

Thoreau once wrote, "The mass of men lead lives of quiet desperation." It would be presumptuous of me to say those people in the park were leading such lives, but I sometimes find myself thinking that. Right or wrong, sometimes when I see them, I think that.

Life is about choices. Choose wisely. If we do not choose, then life chooses for us.

It's never too late to be who you might have been.

George Eliot (1819–1880)
English writer

Our Friends and Family

We will be known forever by the tracks we leave.

Native American proverb (Dakota tribe)

The only thing

Some of the best stories I heard came from asking people about their friends and family.

When earlier versions of this book were being proofread, this chapter seemed to elicit some strong emotional responses. Several of my proofreaders said that although they found the stories to be very moving and powerful, they could not help but notice that the mood of this chapter was different from the rest. They said it was a bit . . . darker.

After an especially interesting conversation with one of my proof-readers, I considered making changes to the chapter. Perhaps I could interview even *more* people and look for funnier or happier stories. Maybe I could ask different questions or ignore certain types of responses.

In the end, I decided not to change a thing. After all, when I shook the tree, this is what fell out. If these stories are darker than others in this book, then it is simply a testament to the power and importance of the relationships with our friends and family. If I were to change anything, I would be just as foolish as one of those cartoon characters who, after looking out the window and seeing a train coming right at him, just pulls down the shade and cringes.

Many of us, including myself, tend to view our lives as a series of accomplishments and goals. We rack up lists of achievements, check off boxes, and hope that someone somewhere is keeping score. It's hard to remember that our *real* place in this world is with our friends and family. Not at work, and not off by ourselves, but with those who know us best.

Although we tend to think in terms of what our friends and family can give us or what they mean to us, our happiness seems to hinge on what we do for them, or what we *should* have done but failed to do. We will forgive ourselves many things, but we usually do not forgive ourselves if we let down the ones we love.

It turns out that those I interviewed learned a lot from the people in their lives. They learned how to be, and sometimes how not to be. When asked, some of them said they would give *anything* just for one chance to go back and do things differently.

It is in this chapter where the whispers are the loudest.

 # Sinners and saints
(Gloria, advertising executive, 42)

This is going to haunt me till the day I die.

When I was growing up, my family had some money and most of my girlfriends at school came from the same type of background. We considered ourselves to be a pretty tight-knit group. Whether it was shopping, socializing, or just taking advantage of what the city had to offer, we did a lot together.

One of the girls I knew in college was a tiny little thing named Tina. We were roommates for a while. She was a bit loud and maybe a bit more spoiled than the rest of us. For whatever reason, despite the fact that she really tried, she just never quite fit in.

There was one weekend when I invited all of my school friends to spend the night at my parents' house out on Long Island. Everyone was invited. Everyone, that is, except Tina. I excluded her because I *knew* the other girls didn't like her. The peer pressure was strong. Their approval was very important to me.

Somehow Tina found out about my little gathering. She drove all the way out to my parents' house and showed up unannounced. I had no idea what to do, so I let her spend the day with us.

My girlfriends did *not* make Tina feel welcome. They rolled their eyes at her, talked about her behind her back; they didn't even *pretend* to like her. As the hostess, I felt like I had to do something.

When it got late, Tina asked if she could stay over instead of driving all the way home. I *froze* when she asked me that. I knew how long a drive she had, but I was worried about what everyone else would say. Against what my heart told me and despite the fact that I knew it was wrong, I said no.

I told her that since there were so many people staying over, there just wasn't enough room. I lied to her. My parents' house was *huge*. There would have been plenty of room.

The look on her face when she left my house *still* haunts me. That was terrible. *I* was terrible.

Tina and I didn't see too much of each other after that. I was so embarrassed and ashamed of what I did that I tended to avoid her. Whenever we did run into each other, I'd give her a thin smile and a polite wave, but that was about it. Things were pretty awkward between us.

It's strange how the world turns. Five years later, when my older sister was dying of cancer, Tina was the *only* one of my friends to visit us in the hospital. She even brought a gift too.

The look on my face must have shown my appreciation, or at least I hope it did. My sister was dying and I just didn't have a clear enough head to apologize to Tina. All I remember was feeling really grateful to her and *really* ashamed of myself. After I had been so cruel, she still found it in her heart to be there for me. It was a very considerate and selfless thing that she did. I've never forgotten it.

The gift Tina brought was an expensive gift basket from one of those specialty stores. One of the things in the basket was a bottle of my sister's favorite perfume. Now whenever I smell that perfume, I don't think of my sister right away. First, I think of Tina.

> *To make no mistake is not in the power of man;*
> *but from their errors and mistakes the wise and*
> *the good learn wisdom for the future.*
>
> Plutarch (46–120)
> Greek historian and philosopher

 # Ramifications
(Hugh, government employee, 59)

I wanted to get married when I was 17 years old. When I told my parents they said, "Great. Go ahead," so I did. It turned out to be a complete disaster.

My parents weren't bad parents. They were just very down-to-earth, simple people who didn't know any better. They didn't have much in the way of an education and that affected how they saw the world.

It's kind of a shame because I sure could've used some good advice, but they didn't have any to give. "Are you sure that this is the right thing to do? Have you thought about the long-term ramifications of this?" Anything like that might have helped.

Sure, I still might have said, "Well, what do *you* know?" and gone ahead and gotten married anyway, but at least I would've heard a different viewpoint. It would have been something to slow me, to stop me for a moment and make me think.

During the *first* year, my marriage was in serious trouble. I had absolutely no business getting married at that age. I didn't know how to handle marriage or what to expect. I hate using such an old cliché, but I never had a chance to sow my wild oats, so it was just a disaster.

My wife and I had two daughters within the first two years. I left when they were both very small. My immaturity, plus the fact that the divorce turned out to be very bitter, kept me away from my kids. I hardly saw the two of them after I left.

About 16 years later, when they were around 17 and 18, the two of them came and sought me out. We started talking on the phone, planning a few get-togethers, whatever we could do. We've been struggling to find some common ground ever since.

When they first sought me out, I wanted to spend more time with them, but things were a little complicated. By then, I was in a new marriage. My new wife and I then adopted a five-month-old baby. I couldn't just drop what I was doing with my new wife and baby to spend the day with my two other daughters. My time was spoken for.

By that time, I knew that I had made big mistakes with my daughters, but if I didn't devote myself to my new family, I knew I'd just be making the same mistakes all over again. I had to choose between trying to make amends with my teenage daughters or trying to do things right the first time with my new family. I chose my new family.

Now my daughters are in their late thirties and they've got kids of their own. They say that they don't resent me for everything that happened, but they must. How can they not? That's got to mark you in a way that you just don't get over. I think growing up without a father definitely affected the way they turned out. They're both a little . . . unstable.

We talk on the phone and get together around the holidays, but there's definitely something missing. There's always a gap between us that never gets bridged. We just can't seem to get there.

Who ever stops to think that what they do when they're young will have such an effect on other people? Of all of the things in my life that I wish I could go back and do differently, number one on the list would be how I handled the relationship with my daughters. Yeah, I wish I hadn't gotten married so young, but that's not really it. I wasn't a part of my daughters' lives when they were kids, when they really needed me.

That's something that, no matter what I do now, I can't change. Those are the kinds of things that really hurt when you sit and think about them. It's like if you caused a really bad car accident where other people were hurt or killed. If it wasn't a random thing, but something *you* did, if you were drinking or negligent, there's no escaping it. There's nothing more painful than a fact or a condition that you know there's no changing.

> *This only is denied to God: the power to undo the past.*
>
> Agathon (448–400 B.C.)
> Greek poet

How cavalier
(Chris, small business owner, 40)

My friend Antoine was the only other guy in school who could play guitar really well. That's how we first met. We started hanging out together and became best friends. We just got along great.

We used to hang out, play guitars, smoke pot, listen to music, and drive around in my car. Although Antoine never used to do any, I did a lot of coke. I didn't have an addictive personality, so it did have its limits. What I mean is that I never ended up getting involved with it to the point where I thought about selling my car to buy coke.

Antoine had this fear of coke. I don't really know where it came from or what it was all about, but he just wouldn't try it. For a long time, I didn't bug him about it, but I'll never forget the night that I *did* bug him about it. We were both about 21. We were over my house, up in my bedroom. I was an adult, but I was living in the bedroom that I grew up in, so it was kind of a weird space.

I cut a line of coke for him on this little white card table that I had set up next to my bed. I really pushed him hard to try some, but he was tentative. I can still see him, hunched over that rickety card table with a rolled-up dollar bill in his hand. I egged him on. I teased him. I called him a pussy. I didn't let up until he did it.

The following week, we did some more. It became a regular thing for the two of us. He got really into it. Fast forward to a year later: he was a full-blown coke addict. We hardly saw each other after that. Five years later, I didn't even know where he was. Nobody did.

Since then, I've searched the Internet, the phone book, classmate websites, and everything else I can think of. I've called everybody who ever knew him. Nobody seems to know anything. The only thing I haven't done yet is hire a private investigator, but I will. I've got to find out what happened to him.

The worst thing about it is that I can't say that the whole thing was innocent. I can't plead ignorance. I was 21 and the fact that I used coke and Antoine didn't, *that* made me feel like a big man. *I* was an adult. *I* did coke. Holding that over him made me feel important. The fact that he was leery of the whole thing just made him seem more like a child and me more like an adult.

When I look back, I can't believe how cavalier I was about pushing coke on him. I don't think that anybody ever stops to think about what sway they may hold over other people. You don't realize how easily you can affect someone's life until something extreme happens.

Antoine was a gentle guy. He was a musician, an artist. I've got to find out what happened to him. It'll kill me if I find out that I ruined that guy's life.

An insincere and evil friend is more to be feared than
a wild beast; a wild beast may wound your body,
but an evil friend will wound your mind.

Buddha

Emotional ice cube
(Vivian, corporate manager, 38)

When I was growing up, my house was always the "hang out" house. My mom was a great hostess and she always made my friends feel very comfortable. Despite the fact that my mom was great to all of my friends, there never seemed to be any joy in it for her. There never seemed to be any joy in *anything* that she did. She was happy being unhappy, if you know what I mean.

My mom was a hard person to talk to. The truth is, no one really talked with my mother. *She* talked and *you* listened. If you didn't, you paid the price.

My mom was so intimidating that I usually ended up doing whatever she said. She bullied me into going to the college that *she* wanted, taking the major that *she* wanted me to take, and finally, going into the career that *she* wanted for me. Looking back, I can't believe how passive and subservient I was. I guess when it's your mother and it's all you know, you go along for the ride.

She wasn't a bad person; it's just the way she was raised. Her parents were very cold, angry, and contentious people. They were always ready to pick a fight. I know because they lived with us for many years.

My mom spent her whole life trying in vain to earn the approval of her parents. Standing in our kitchen years ago, I heard my mother say to my grandfather, "Dad, you've never said that you were proud of me." My grandfather's response was, "Well, if you ever do anything I'm proud of, I'll let you know." Can you believe it? I was so heartbroken for my mom.

My grandparents behaved in ways that I always thought were very strange. They demanded that they be the center of attention at all times. It didn't matter where they were or what was going on, the world revolved around them. It was the weirdest thing.

At age 52, my mom developed lung cancer. Even when everyone

knew she was dying, even when she was hospitalized, everything *still* revolved around her parents. I remember my mother being all upset and trying to get out of her hospital bed because her dad wanted a cup of coffee. As his daughter lay dying, my grandfather still thought that he was the most important person in the room. Imagine being *that* guy's daughter.

It was only after my mom got sick that I began to understand her. When I was growing up, I remember thinking that my parents were in a totally different class. I thought that they were infallible, that they always had all of the answers. My mom's illness allowed me to see her not so much as my mother, but as a little girl whose parents didn't tell her that they loved her. After that, I had a lot of sympathy for her.

To the end, my mom was an iron woman. When the end *did* come, I was sitting next to her in her hospital room, holding her hand. With her eyes closed, she squeezed my hand and said, "I don't want to d-i-e." And then she did. She couldn't even say the word; she had to spell it. Her parents had turned her into such an emotional ice cube that she couldn't feel anything.

I was 25 when my mom died. I was very confused because it was the first time in my life that I didn't have someone telling me what to do. I was a grown woman, but I was lost.

Later that year when I got my own apartment, I had to call my sister to help me decorate it. I didn't even know what I liked or what my tastes were. My mother had always decorated my dorm rooms or my off-campus apartments for me. I always grew up thinking that I was *so* independent. It was a real eye-opener for me. It was pretty embarrassing, too.

You can't try to be everything to your kids. You can't think for them, you can't decide everything for them. It's just not healthy. If you treat your kids like children their whole lives, they'll grow up to be children. They'll just be kids in adult bodies.

It's a strange thing to say, but if my mother were still alive, I'm sure that we wouldn't be speaking. I would have stood up to her by now and that would have been the end of it. If I had stood up to my mother when I was younger, maybe my life would have taken another direction. At 38 years old, I'm changing careers and I finally feel like I'm on the right path. For the first time in my life, I feel like things are all right.

> *To know everything is to forgive everything.*
>
> Germaine de Staël (1766–1817)
> French-Swiss novelist

 # Iron men
(Ted, financial planner, 40)

My dad used to do a lot of name calling. He was what you might call an "old school" type of dad. He wasn't a bad guy, but he never knew the impact that his words had on me.

My dad would drag my self-esteem down whenever he got angry. Whenever I'd make a mistake, he'd tear into me by calling me a moron, an idiot, or stupid. For example, when I was about 11 years old, he took a day off from work to watch me play football. I was out there playing my best, but I guess my dad thought that I wasn't trying hard enough.

When the game was over, right in front of everybody, he called me every name in the book. He was seriously pissed off because he said that he wasted a personal day just to watch me screw up. He put me down like that all the time.

Yeah, they were just words, but try to remember what your world was like when you were a kid. Kids idolize their parents. When you hear your parents call you names or any time they insult you, you really feel that. You take it to heart. When your parents put you down, you start to believe it.

Having thought about it for my whole life, I decided that even if my kid *was* a knucklehead, I would never call him a knucklehead. Not ever.

Now I have a son of my own. When he screws up, as all kids do, I address his behavior, *not* who he is as a person. We talk about whatever we need to talk about and I don't put him down.

I give him what I call the "crap sandwich." First I say something nice, then I address the problem, and then I end it with something nice. That way, the crap is in the middle. The first and last things that he hears from me are always supportive.

Just like I used to, my son plays football. I go to his games to support him and to show him that I love him. When I'm there, I sometimes see other dads yelling and screaming at their kids. Earlier in the season, there was this one clown who was yelling at his kid, but he was also yelling at everyone else's kids too. By the end of the second game, I had had enough of that guy. I walked over and whispered a little something to him. He kept his mouth shut after that.

The thing is this: I don't walk around feeling sorry for myself because my dad used to yell at me. He just didn't know any better. Maybe that's how he was raised. Maybe that's who he was or who he became; I don't know. It doesn't really matter. All that matters is that I knew I wouldn't treat *my* son that way.

*Life is a grindstone, and whether it
grinds a man down or polishes him up
depends on the stuff he's made of.*

Josh Billings (1818–1885)
American humorist and lecturer

A note for my mother
(Dorothy, professional musician, 35)

The relationship that I have with my mom is great . . . *now*. My mom was not easy to live with, but I look back now and I'm grateful. She kept me grounded. She didn't fight with me because she was a bad person; she just wanted me to have a better life. She was very tough on me and always made me do the right thing. Now I'm glad that she was tough.

If it hadn't been for my mother, I would have dropped out of college. I remember the night that I called her and told her I couldn't handle it. It was raining like crazy and I was in tears standing in one of my dorm's outdoor phone booths. I was failing many of my classes and I didn't understand why.

My mom had a high school education. As a single mother who raised two children, she knew firsthand how difficult it was for a woman without an education to survive. She emphasized the *absolute need* for me to stay in school. She was not going to let me make the same mistakes that she made.

My mom had never driven off of Long Island before, let alone through New York City. The thought of driving through Manhattan *terrified* her. But that rainy night, she drove through the city and for three more hours north to my school just to keep me from dropping out. *That's* the kind of relationship we have.

Now that I'm older, my mom and I are much closer. We've got so much more in common. We're both mothers and we're both very involved in my son's life. We don't live too far away from each other, so we get together constantly. Over time, we've also developed a lot of the same values. I think that we have a mutual respect for each other now. I have a lot of relatives with kids who are my son's age, but if something ever happens to me and my husband, my mom is going to take custody of my son.

They say that people who go through hardships or bad times together develop strong connections. That really applies to me and my mother. When I was about six years old, my father died. My mom took it very hard. She went out and got a job and tried to support us as best she could, but most times we didn't have enough money to meet the bills. She'd come home from work every night looking like she was carrying the weight of the world on her shoulders. Sometimes she seemed really beaten down.

Because I was only a little kid, I didn't know how to help her. The only thing I could think of was to leave my mom little notes. So every night, I'd write my mom a note. I'd put it on her pillow before bed.

In these notes, I'd tell my mom how I felt about her. I'd tell her that she was a good mom and a great person. To this day, we have never said a word to each other about those notes.

Just last year, I went looking for something in a stack of papers that my mom kept in her dresser drawer. When I got to the bottom of the pile, there they were—the notes that I had written to her. She had saved them all. Can you imagine that? All those years later, she still had my notes.

Magic hour
(Kelly, licensed practical nurse, 61)

When my husband and I decided to start a family, we were prepared mentally, but not financially. I'm glad that we went ahead and did it anyway. We were blessed with four beautiful daughters, but if we had waited until we could afford it, we would only have one! The truth is that if you plan a little, you'll always get by.

Motherhood was the best thing that ever happened to me. For as long as I can remember, I've always wanted to be a mother. My daughters are such a blessing to me.

My daughters are all grown now, but I still think about the days when they were little and we all lived together. I remember all those summer afternoons when the girls had their friends over. They'd all be running around outside. There'd be toys in the yard and bikes in the driveway. The sun would start to go down and that beautiful orange light would cover everything. I'd look around and say, "Thank God. This is where I belong."

> *Yes, there is a Nirvana: it is in leading your sheep to a green pasture, and in putting your child to sleep, and in writing the last line of your poem.*

> Kahlil Gibran (1883–1931)
> Lebanese American author and artist

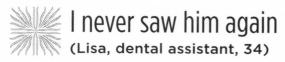

I never saw him again
(Lisa, dental assistant, 34)

One day, some 18-year-old girl showed up at our door and told my mother that she and my father were in love and that they were going to run off together. Well, sure enough, they did. My father walked away without even talking to my brother and me. I was about ten years old.

My anger at him got worse after I became a mother. I thought, *My god, how can you run out on your kids? How can you not fight for your children?* Sometimes I feel bad that I can't forgive him, but I just can't. As I get older, it gets harder.

After my son was born, I decided to let my father see him. I *still* didn't want anything to do with my father, but I didn't want my son to grow up never knowing his grandfather. My father and I speak on the phone once in a while, but my husband is the one who takes my son to see him. It's been almost 24 years and I still can't bring myself to visit him.

My anger towards my father is the biggest reason for refusing to see him, but a part of me refuses because of my loyalty to my mother. Do you want to know the funniest part of this whole thing? *She's* the one who's been encouraging me to forgive him. Weird, isn't it?

Regarding this situation with my father, my biggest regret has to do with my paternal grandfather. He was the best. I really loved him.

After my father left, we didn't get to see my grandfather anymore. I don't really remember if it was because we took sides or if it was because he did. All I know is that I never saw him again.

He passed away 13 years ago. Right before he died, I called him and we talked for a long time. I'm really glad I did that. He really was the best.

I regret those lost years.

# A strong son
(Anthony, department store manager, 46)

My parents were heavy drinkers when I was a kid. Even though I was really young, I still remember the two of them coming home late, being kind of loud and sloppy. They were rarely "angry drunks," they were usually very happy when they were like that. Even so, it was still embarrassing.

One night, I remember my parents coming home from a house party down the street. As usual, they had been drinking heavily. I was ten years old and was sitting at the table doing a homework assignment on magnets and magnetism. With a wave and a big smile, my father came over to the kitchen table to see what I was doing. He wobbled a little as he stood behind me and looked over my shoulder at the homework.

My homework page was covered with small drawings of magnets. Each magnet was labeled with a "north" and a "south" end. It was my job to look at each diagram and, using my basic knowledge of magnets, decide whether or not the two magnets in each drawing would attract each other or repel each other.

My father took a quick look at the answers I had written down so far. Although the teacher had reviewed the material in class and I understood the assignment, my father began telling me that I was doing it all wrong. He loudly told me that opposites repel one another. He said that it was the ends of the magnets that were the same that would attract each other. When I told him that the teacher had taught me something completely different, he said that the teacher was wrong.

Even though I knew that he had been drinking, it never occurred to me that my father could be wrong. He was never wrong; he was my father. I immediately changed all of my answers.

The next day in class, the teacher called on me to review some of the homework answers. Of course, I had every single one wrong. The teacher *knew* that I was a good student and he remembered reviewing it with me in class the day before, so he was a bit surprised at my mistakes. I politely told the teacher that I hadn't made any mistakes. I told the teacher that although I remembered the lesson, my father had taught me how magnets *really* worked. Some of the other kids in class giggled and I started to feel a bit uncomfortable.

The teacher picked up on my embarrassment and quietly took me to the back of the classroom. He showed me a table where he had set up several magnets. He quietly demonstrated that opposite ends of the magnets attract, not the same ends, as my father had told me.

As I shuffled back to my seat, I felt a little ashamed. It was only a homework assignment, but I felt that I was seeing my father for the first time and it embarrassed me. When my father would tell me that he knew this or that, I always believed him. I always knew that he had a drinking problem, but it had never really affected me before that day.

Even though that incident with my father took place over 30 years ago, to this day I drink socially, but I never allow myself to drink to excess. Now that I'm a father, my children mean the world to me and I would never risk putting them in any situation in which they might be ashamed or embarrassed by me. What my children think of me is one of the most important things in my life. I will never let my children see me the way my father let me see him.

A child's life is like a piece of paper
on which every person leaves a mark.

Chinese proverb

My mentor
(Claire, customer service agent, 63)

If I could do things over, I'd be a lot easier on my daughter. We fought *a lot*. At the time, I thought I was helping her, but I was unnecessarily rough on her.

She had a weight problem when she was younger and I treated her differently because of it. In our house, we always had dessert after dinner. After everyone was done, I'd usually say something like this to my husband and my son: "Who wants more ice cream?" But I wouldn't say it to my daughter. Yes, it's a small thing, but I was saying something without saying it. I think that there are some wounds there.

My daughter and I used to fight about her school work, too. My son was the academic star of the family. Whenever I went to those parent/teacher conference nights, *I* became the star. They all said, "Oh, you're *Stan's* mother?! He's *so* wonderful!" The teachers all thought that I was such a fantastic mother because my son was such a fantastic student. I thrived on that attention.

When my daughter started school a few years later, things changed. My daughter was just an average student, but because I wasn't getting the adoration from the teachers anymore, I rode her for it. It became more about me than it was about her. It took me a while to figure out that those were *my* shortcomings, not hers.

Since then, we've talked a lot about those things and I think she's okay with what happened. She's *my* mentor now. She's kind, she's a great mother, and she's got a great perspective on things. She's really turned out to be very special.

Courage
(Nick, physical therapist, 34)

Last Christmas, my mother-in-law threw a party for the whole family. After dinner, she handed out cards to everybody. The cards looked like regular Christmas cards on the outside, but when we opened them we saw that there was nothing on the inside except a single word that she had handwritten. Everyone's card had a different word in it.

We went around the table and everyone had to read their word out loud. While I was waiting for my turn, I just sat there staring at my card. I started to feel really self-conscious. I started to get a lump in my throat.

By the time my turn came, I was teary-eyed and couldn't really speak. I sort of gestured to my wife who was sitting next to me and showed her my card. My wife saw that I was in a jam, so she bailed me out. She's the best. She distracted everyone by saying something that I can't remember right now. Then she leaned over, took a look at my card and said, "All right everybody, Nick's word is . . . *courage*." Everybody went, "Ahhh" and then we continued to go around the table.

I excused myself and stepped outside to get my act together. *That* was pretty embarrassing. A minute or two later, my wife came over to see how I was doing. Everything was under control, and after a few deep breaths, I was ready to get back inside.

I know it's really stupid, but the word in my card reminded me of something that happened between me and my dad. My dad was a big-hearted guy, but he was also a little eccentric. He liked to talk a lot, and sometimes he alienated people.

When I was a teenager, I went to work with my dad once and I spent the whole day with him at his job site. Unfortunately, I also spent the day with two of my dad's co-workers. They were a couple of disgusting looking guys. They looked like two skinny little drug addicts with really bad teeth.

All day, those guys kept making fun of my dad. Sometimes they did it to his face and sometimes behind his back, but always so that I could hear. Those guys made me mad, but I didn't say anything. I didn't stick up for my dad.

That must have been 19 years ago, but it still bothers me that I didn't have the courage to say something to those guys. He was my dad, for God's sake. A son should stand up for his father. It's a little open-ended for me because my dad's gone now and I can't tell him about it and square it with him.

You know, I never told *anybody* that story about my dad. And then my mother-in-law hits me with that card. I kept thinking, *How did she know? How the hell did she know?* That's why I got so choked up. I figured that everybody could see through me, like I wore it on my face or something. "There's Nick. He didn't have the courage to stick up for his dad."

I still haven't told my mother-in-law why I got so upset. I just decided to take the experience as a sign to live my life with more courage. That's all.

Carry that weight
(Andy, mechanic, 35)

Unfortunately, I'm carrying several grudges right now. All of them are due to pride. They're a complete waste of energy.

The one that's going on now with my dad is torturing me. His new wife is coming between us. She and I had an argument over a Christmas card. Yeah, a Christmas card. My dad's taken her side in the whole thing and I haven't spoken to him in over a year.

The worst thing about it is history seems to be repeating itself. My dad and my grandfather weren't speaking in the months before my grandfather died. My dad really regrets that. You'd think that we'd learn, but we don't.

> *He that cannot forgive others breaks the*
> *bridge over which he must pass himself;*
> *for every man has need to be forgiven.*

George Herbert (1593–1633)
English poet

I can't remember
(Donna, retired court stenographer, 69)

I'm an alcoholic. I've been one for the past 32 years. The good news is that I've been a recovering alcoholic for the last 27 of those 32 years. The bad news is that I was a complete drunk for the first five.

I'm not really sure how or when my alcoholism got started. That sort of thing is insidious. You just don't wake up one day and decide to become a drunk. It's the sort of thing that sneaks up on you.

It was when I was about 37 years old that things began to unravel. For me, it probably came down to a lack of self-worth. At the time, my husband was working two jobs. We had five kids. On top of all that, I was a perfectionist. I just couldn't manage.

As my alcoholism got worse, my life got more and more out of control. I really let myself go. I was forgetting important things and my kids began to suffer.

For example, I forgot to pick up my five-year-old daughter from school one day. All of the other kids were long gone and she just stood there and cried. She waited for hours until the school could get a hold of my husband. God, I don't even know where I *was* that day.

My husband was the first one to try to help me with my drinking problem. There were no such things as interventions back then, but that's pretty much what he did. In subtle and sometimes not so subtle ways, he made me face my alcoholism. He kept on me until I agreed to get help. He was right, but I really resented him at the time.

When I first went to counseling, I was living with a tremendous amount of guilt. The guilt of letting my family down—my husband, and especially my kids—was like a weight on my back. Counseling helped me to get over the guilt. My kids were a big help to me too. They reassured me and said that I *had* been there for them. They said I *hadn't* let them down.

My younger kids don't remember all of the things I did when I was drunk, but the older ones do. Even I don't remember everything, but what I do remember is pretty awful. My husband has filled in some of the gaps in my memory with lots of stories about yelling and hitting. There are things that I just can't tell you. It's too embarrassing.

The things I did and said back then were pretty bad. Aside from being very ashamed and embarrassed, I can't help but wonder and worry if I've caused my kids irreparable damage. I'll never really know if that's true or not, but I've got to live with that.

It's been 27 years since my last drink. Twenty-seven years clean.

Children might or might not be a blessing,
but to create them and then fail them
was surely damnation.

Lois McMaster Bujold (1949–)
American author

Her life
(Angela, receptionist, 49)

One of the things I wish I had done was to ask my mom about her life. My mom was widowed at a young age and she really had a tough time. I knew about some of it, but I never knew the whole story. I was too afraid of bringing up hurtful memories, so I never asked. It's not that she told me never to ask her, I just always had the feeling that it was a taboo subject. I guess I sort of put limits on myself.

One day, Mom and I found a box of her old stuff in the attic. We brought it down to her bedroom and went through it. There were some pictures in there, old clothes, some letters—things like that. We were halfway through the box when she suddenly froze up. I'll never forget the look on her face. She just sort of stopped talking, sat on the bed, and stared out the window for a long time.

Whenever there was a moment like that, or whenever she would say a little something about her past, I never said, "Hey Ma, tell me more about that." I just ignored it. I just didn't have the guts.

Now that she's gone, I'm sorry that I didn't at least try. Not just for my sake, but for hers too. What if she wanted to tell me, but didn't know how to start? Would it have made it easier for her if she could have unloaded some of that on me? Could I have helped her in some way? She's gone now and it's too late.

> *The bitterest tears shed over graves are for*
> *words left unsaid and deeds left undone.*

Harriet Beecher Stowe (1811–1896)
American writer

Friend to a friend
(Helen, homemaker, 42)

I have great friends now, but because I turned my back on so many of the friends I had when I was younger, I had to start over again as an adult. It's hard to see the importance of some things when you're young.

Back when I first started high school, I had an amazing group of friends that I hung out with constantly. We did *everything* together. There was Stephanie, Tina, Joanne, who was *hysterical*, Patti, Vicki, and me.

Friday nights were our big nights out. We'd all pile into Tina's father's car and go to this place called Ronny's. It was a restaurant that stayed open late on the weekends. Sometimes they had live music. As long as we kept ordering food, they let us hang out at our corner table for hours. That place wasn't much to look at, but God, we had great times there.

One night at Ronny's, Joanne became *infamous* for this hilarious stunt she pulled. She stood in front of the jukebox and wouldn't let anyone pick any songs. She'd take their money and then *she'd sing the songs for them.* We were *dying* laughing. She kept it up until the owner came out and asked her to stop.

Our Friday night ritual lasted for quite a while. Even after I started hanging out with my boyfriend, nothing got in the way of going to "Ronny's." Friday nights were for my girlfriends; Saturday nights were for my boyfriend. That was it.

Eventually, I started getting more serious with my boyfriend and he wanted to start seeing me on Friday nights too. My friends kept calling me to see if I wanted to go out with them, but I started brushing them off. I've got to give them credit; they kept calling me for *months* before they gave up. Joanne was the last holdout, but even her calls slowed down until finally they stopped all together.

At the time, I didn't care that I had abandoned all of my girlfriends. I was very immature. It's a shame because I really had a lot of good friends back then. Thinking about it really bothers me now.

My mother warned me not to make that mistake. She tried to tell me how important my friends would be to me, but I didn't understand. She always said, "Helen, your girlfriends are your girlfriends *for life*." I couldn't see it at the time, but it's true. It's always been that way for *my* mother. She's had some of the same friends for over 50 years.

In my late twenties, I made a conscious effort to be a better friend. You can't just wish or pray for friends; you have to be one first before you can have one. I *decided* to have new friends. When I got them, I decided that *this time*, I would appreciate them.

Now, as an adult, I have wonderful friends. They're friends who've been there through good times and bad times. They were there for my family and me when my husband was sick. We're always helping each other out and doing favors for one another. Sometimes we even pick each other's kids up from school or soccer practice or whatever.

If I could do things over, I'd respect and appreciate the importance of friendship. When I was younger, I had to go through a lot of important things by myself because I had alienated all of my girlfriends.

The only way to have a friend is to be one.

Ralph Waldo Emerson (1803–1882)
American essayist

For my grandmother
(Laura, mental health counselor, 26)

My mother was really manipulative. She was very self-centered and extremely jealous of *any* attention that my father would show me. She once said, "Before you came along, your father used to pay attention to *me*. Now everything is Laura, Laura, Laura!"

The weirdest thing about my mother was that she didn't get along with anyone. She didn't like any of my aunts, uncles, grandparents— nobody. She badmouthed them all, but she attacked my dad's mother the hardest. She used to tell me these ridiculous stories about how my grandmother mistreated my dad when he was a kid.

Just like my mother wanted, I learned to hate all of the people that my mother hated, especially my dad's mother. I became a very bitter and angry little kid. I was too young to recognize my mother for who she was or what she was doing, so I believed everything she told me.

Every Christmas, my dad's mother had everybody over to her house for dinner. She really bent over backwards to make it nice. She'd cook a big meal and hand out presents to everyone. She'd always set something up special for me, like a new dollhouse or something like that, but I ignored the gifts she tried to give me. I ignored her too.

After dinner, she would ask me if I wanted to help her in the kitchen with dessert. I used to just walk off and not even answer her. That always embarrassed my dad a lot. He tried to get me to do or say something nice, but I wouldn't.

When I was about nine years old, my dad's mother died. I had always been mean to her, so her death really didn't affect me. She meant nothing to me.

About seven years later, when I was 16 years old, I got a letter from my grandfather. In the letter, he told me that he was so disappointed in me. He said that all that my grandmother ever wanted was for me to love her. All she ever wanted was for me to put my arms around her and hug her. She really loved me and the fact that I never showed her any affection really tore her up inside.

My grandfather's letter devastated me. By that age, I had already figured out who my mother was and how she manipulated me. I knew the truth. I knew that my mother had lied about so many things.

I had treated my grandmother so terribly. I was cruel to her. I had been so wrong, but there was nothing I could do. She was dead. There are no words to describe the guilt and the pain that I felt.

Since that time, I have tried to mend fences with as many of my relatives as I can. They all understand what happened and they seem to forgive me. Things are pretty good now between all of us, but I think that any chance for a close relationship with any of them is gone. I guess I have to live with that.

Turning my back on my grandmother is one of the deepest regrets of my life. The worst thing about it is that I can't undo it. No amount of tears, no amount of wishing or praying can change it. There's no letter I can write, no one I can call. It just is.

I treat everyone differently now.

No matter how far you have gone
on a wrong road, turn back.

Turkish proverb

Chinks in the armor

Early on in this process, I did not have a refined list of questions nor did I have a system in place to look for potential interviewees.

Not knowing what else to do, I began testing out some of my interview questions on the captains with whom I flew.

For several months, I gave it my best shot. I explained the purpose of the book and described what it was that I was looking for, but all I got were a lot of blank stares and plain vanilla answers. It was not an encouraging start.

It then occurred to me that the captains I tried to interview were poor subjects not because they had nothing to say, but because of who they had to be in order to *be* captains. Decades of military discipline coupled with the weight of the responsibilities carried by airline captains had made many of them a bit detached and inaccessible. By and large, they considered themselves to be people who didn't make mistakes, who didn't look back. For a time, I thought that I would never find any holes in their curtains, any chinks in their armor.

All of that changed one night after a fairly long day of flying. All that day, the captain with whom I was working had been a good sport by listening to my interview questions, but as usual, I had absolutely no luck with him. Back then, there was not much subtlety to the questions I asked; they were rather one-dimensional. In one form or another, I kept asking him if there was anything in his life that he would have liked to have done differently. The only response I got was a slow shake of the head and a laconic, "Nope." I eventually gave up.

Later that evening after we had finished eating dinner, we walked back to the hotel in silence. The captain had not talked much during dinner and I was a bit concerned that something was wrong. It had been hours since I had asked him my interview questions, but I was about to find out that he had not stopped thinking about them. He finally broke the silence and told me this story.

 # Gone fishing
(Dale, airline pilot, 58)

The summer that my boy turned ten years old, he became very interested in fishing. One of his friends and his friend's dad were doing a lot of father/son stuff and I guess my boy thought that fishing would be something he and I could do together. I didn't think it was such a great idea, but I said, "Okay, D.J. Whatever."

The night before every one of my days off, he'd ask me if I wanted to go fishing the next morning. We went out about two or three times in July, but as far as he was concerned, not often enough. I just wasn't interested in going.

We didn't go out at all during the month of August. Towards the end of the summer, my boy started getting a little edgy. He was pretty upset that the summer was ending and that we hadn't done much fishing. I promised him that we'd go out at least one more time before he started school.

Our last chance to go fishing came during the Labor Day weekend. He tried to wake me up each morning, but I kept telling him no. I pushed it off at first by telling him that we'd go tomorrow, but by the third morning, we had run out of tomorrows.

He really tried to get me out of bed that third morning, but I just wouldn't. He kept saying, "But you promised." I just didn't want to get up early, so that was that. We didn't go.

My boy's an adult now. We haven't spoken in almost three years. The reasons don't really matter. It's got nothing to do with this. The funny thing is, not a week goes by that I don't think about how I broke my promise to him. All he wanted to do was spend some time with me, you know?

You wanted to know if there was anything in my life that I wish I could have done differently. Well, I wish I had gotten out of bed and gone fishing with my son.

We are always too busy for our children;
we never give them the time or interest they deserve.
We lavish gifts upon them; but the most precious gift,
our personal association, which means
so much to them, we give grudgingly.

Mark Twain (1835–1910)
American writer, humorist, and lecturer

Relationships, Love,
and Marriage

I wouldn't presume

Since the invention of the campfire, people have told stories about love and relationships. A few thousand years later, along came the printing press, which enabled us to read about them as well. Whether they appear in weekly magazines, newspaper advice columns, or romance novels, stories about love and relationships are perhaps the most popular things in print today. In fact, so much has been written about this subject that I have decided not to add my editorial comments to the heap.

Here are several stories given to me by my interviewees that represent realizations and moments of decision that transformed their lives. When asked, they honestly discussed the mistakes they made, the things they would have done differently, and the victories that their persistence and experience brought them.

A borrowed man
(Cindy, corporate manager, 35)

No one ever says, "When I grow up, I'm going to have an affair with a married man," but that's what I ended up doing. It's not something I'm proud of, but it is what happened. For seven years, I was involved with a married man. I do *not* recommend it.

We first met when we were both around 16 years old. We were very different, but we really cared about each other. We were each other's first love.

We broke up and went our separate ways while we were still in school. After graduation, we just didn't see each other much. Years later, we bumped into each other. We said hello and gave each other a hug. We started talking on a regular basis. I guess you could say that we became friends again.

Because we were older and there were no silly school-age pressures on us anymore, we were able to really talk, to really tell each other what we thought and how we felt. A few of these honest conversations revealed that we had broken up because of some misunderstandings. It turned out that we still had strong feelings for each other. It didn't take long for us to begin our affair.

He worked in the same general area that I did, so we used to meet at lunchtime and after work. These clandestine meetings and our little secret lives actually seemed normal after a while. We kept it up for years.

About three and a half years into the affair, I decided that I needed a change. I moved a few hundred miles away and tried to get a little distance on the situation. It seemed to work for a while, but we ended up continuing the affair via the phone lines. There were a lot of teary phone calls and a lot of emotional breakdowns during that time. It was as if I never left.

Running away from my problem did nothing to solve it. I just traded a local problem for a long distance problem; that's all. Wherever and whenever possible, we continued the affair. I eventually returned to be near him.

Your brain can rationalize anything, no matter how wrong or ridiculous it may be, if that rationalization gives you something. Maybe it gives you relief from guilt. Maybe it gives you permission to fail, or to let others down. Whatever stupid stuff you need to convince yourself of, I'm telling you that you can do it. I did it for seven years.

I'll give you a perfect example of what I'm talking about. Right in the middle of my affair, I made friends with a woman who confided in me that she was also seeing a married guy. She told me about how her guy used to badmouth his wife all the time. Her guy complained constantly about how his wife ignored him, how she didn't understand him, the whole thing.

When I heard that, I actually felt good about my situation. I felt superior to her. I remember feeling virtuous because *my* guy never did that. He always told me that *he loved his wife.* Could I have been any dumber?! Do you understand what I'm saying? There is absolutely no sanity in those situations, *none.*

For what it's worth, my guy never did lie to me. He never did say that he was going to leave his wife. As a matter of fact, he never said a bad word about her. He loved her. It was his honesty that kept me ensnared for as long as I was. It would have been easier to break it off if he was some sort of a stereotypical lying, cheating dog, but it wasn't me that he was lying to. He was lying to someone else. And that's the ridiculous and pathetic stuff you cling to when you're as lost as I was.

Being involved in a situation like that wears you down. It makes you angry and bitter and it destroys your self-esteem. When you allow yourself to settle for the crumbs, you begin to unwittingly tell yourself that all you deserve are the crumbs.

My self-esteem got so bad that I eventually had to choose. The options I had were not good ones, but I knew I had to do something. I saw my choices as being: end the relationship (I would lose him; I would give up the man I loved) or stay with him (I would take whatever he was willing to give; I would accept the crumbs).

It wasn't until around my thirtieth birthday that I finally made the right choice. Just because it was the right choice doesn't mean that it was easy. It was one of the hardest things that I've ever had to do, but I did it. I ended the affair. I was really heartbroken.

In hindsight, the whole thing seems to make more sense to me now.

I burned up a big chunk of my twenties going nowhere, emotionally speaking, but now I think I understand why. My life throughout my twenties was completely unstable. I had nothing in my life that was permanent; nothing was mine. I *rented* an apartment. I drove a *company* car. And the man I loved belonged to someone else, too.

I know now that I was afraid to have a real relationship, one with trust and commitment. Part of me was involved in that affair because the expectations were so low. In fact, an affair represents the exact opposite of what a good relationship represents. By the very nature of an affair, there is no trust. There is no commitment. It's perfect for the person who wants nothing because you can never go to the next stage. It's completely safe.

Several years passed and I went through a lot of dark times. I did a lot of growing up too. And then something wonderful happened: I met my fiancé. Meeting him was the best thing that ever happened to me.

The smartest thing I ever did was to say yes to a blind date with him. I had put him off for a year before I agreed to go out with him. Can you imagine? All during that year, I never actually spoke with him. I just kept refusing to give my number to the person who was trying to fix us up. When I finally gave in, when he finally called me, we talked for three hours. We knew so many of the same people and had so much in common, it just fit.

Our relationship works because he makes me comfortable enough to open up to him. I trust him and I can be vulnerable in front of him. We're completely honest with each other.

He knows about the affair I had and he doesn't judge me. He understands that I've changed and grown a lot since then. Now that I have a fiancé, I see the affair from a different perspective. I love my fiancé dearly and I would never do anything like that to him. I just wouldn't.

When it came to men in general, I was always so preoccupied with the wrong things. Because I went to business school in New York City in the 1980s, I always imagined that I'd marry some tall, blond, WASPy bond trader from Wall Street. We'd live in Connecticut and summer in the Hamptons, the whole thing. In all of my daydreams about Mr. Right, I never saw him as being kind, loving, or supportive; I only imagined places and things. What I was really imagining was a life-style, not a life. With my fiancé, I have a life.

My fiancé is not a WASPy bond trader from Wall Street, but somehow he's everything that I've always looked for in a man. I just never looked in the right places before. It's funny how that happens.

> *One word frees us of all the weight*
> *and pain of life: That word is love.*
>
> Sophocles (496–406 B.C.)
> Greek poet

 ## Cyber sex and the Sirens' song
(Steve, architect, 37)

Meeting my wife was a major turning point for me. Before I met her, my life was consumed by bizarre relationships. Quite literally, I had become addicted to Internet dating and cyber sex.

If it hadn't been for a friend of mine, I never would have even *thought* about using my computer to meet women. A guy I had known since grade school told me that he was having phenomenal success meeting women by using the Internet. He amazed me with all of these stories about how he would contact various women via the Internet, make arrangements to meet them, and then have sex with them minutes after they met. I was really intrigued.

After he had convinced me to try this for myself, he added a bit of a warning. Very bluntly he said, "Look, you can do this. This is all very doable, but the women you'll meet are all going to have some problem or something wrong with them. They're all doing this because they feel they have to. If they didn't have some weird problem or characteristic, they wouldn't be willing to do this."

My friend's warning was strong, but it had been quite a while since my last relationship and I was desperate. At that moment, it wouldn't have mattered if those women were serial killers. I jumped right in.

Just as my friend promised, the women were out there. Quickly, I made contact with women from around the country and around the world. Every night after work, I would spend hours on the computer interacting with them.

The type of interaction was different for each woman. Many wanted to type sexually explicit messages back and forth. Others wanted to be able to see me as we interacted. For those women, I bought and set up my own web camera. As you can imagine, I did a lot of things that in hindsight I find quite embarrassing.

Although I thought about and talked about meeting all of these women, the ones who lived within driving distance had priority. I once drove several hundred miles up to Washington State just to meet one of these women. She lived a few hours outside of Spokane, right in the middle of *nowhere*. She wasn't that attractive, but she promised me that if I drove up there we'd have sex. Within minutes of meeting her, she kept her promise.

The scene I just mentioned was played out many times with many different women. On a few occasions, those encounters resulted in unprotected sex. Thankfully I'm disease-free, but I owe that to nothing but dumb luck. My Internet obsession kept putting me in harm's way and it was obvious that I had lost my ability to make good decisions.

Those computer relationships began to color my judgment about other things, too. Things that I would have considered strange at any other time in my life seemed completely normal during those Internet days. For example, on two occasions, I drove hundreds of miles up to

Vancouver, British Columbia. I stayed for three days, but I didn't do any sightseeing. All of my time was spent in the city's strip clubs. On one particularly bad night, I paid a woman to do more than just dance for me.

When I made that trip, I wasn't some teenager; I was a grown man in my mid-thirties. No one thing that I'm telling you is necessarily that bad, but taken as a whole, I think you can see where my life was going. I had completely isolated myself from the real world.

The last straw came one night when I was on a first date with another one of those Internet women. We had met for dinner at a nice restaurant and afterwards, we were getting extremely intimate in the front seat of my car. Right in the middle of fooling around, she burst into tears. Sobbing, she said, "I have a record! I have a record! I was convicted of a federal crime!" She went into details about all of the charges against her and her conviction. She was sentenced to probation. She talked about having to see her parole officer once a week. What a mess.

It was then that I realized that all I was doing was getting myself into one strange and awkward situation after another. I literally spent several hours every day on the computer doing things of which I'm not proud. Every so often, I'd meet one of these strange women and we'd have some sort of a bizarre sexual encounter. After a while, it just felt unhealthy.

Finally I realized that all of the time and effort I was putting into these bizarre relationships could have been better spent looking for a normal woman. That's really what I wanted all along, but couldn't seem to find. Maybe I wasn't looking in the right places. Maybe I wasn't trying hard enough.

It was this change of thinking that changed my life. Instead of my old unproductive behavior, I put myself out into the regular singles arenas and I kept an open mind. I let myself get set up on blind dates. I went to singles mixers. I began to meet real women with real lives.

That's how I met my wife. She's beautiful, she's caring, but most of all, she's *extremely* normal.

I can't believe how much time I wasted running down those dead ends. Luckily for me, it all worked out.

> *I count him braver who overcomes his desires*
> *than him who conquers his enemies;*
> *the hardest victory is the victory over self.*

Aristotle (384–322 B.C.)
Greek philosopher

 # *Love* is a girl's best friend
(Eve, mother/homemaker/small business owner, 42)

I met my first husband when I was 15. When you're young, you should *never* tie yourself to one person. It was a combination of a few things that trapped me in that bad situation.

I was not a good student and because I had no other school activities to take up my time, I devoted *all* of my time to this one guy. He became my world. He went to a different school, so I ended up hanging out with him and all of his friends. His friends were great people, but we became this big dysfunctional group. We all paired off into boy/girl couples and stayed together like that until we got married.

From the time I was 15 to the time I married my first husband, at age 21, I didn't date any other guys. Because I had no other relationships to compare it to, I felt as if I had found true love. What did I know about true love? How could I have known *anything* without dating other people?

I thought that what I felt for him was love, but it wasn't. It was only after I was married for a few years that I realized I didn't love him the way a wife should love her husband. I started having feelings that a married woman shouldn't have. I started catching myself looking at other men. Not just looking, but I'd say, "Wow, he's cute," and I'd start to wonder what it would be like to date him if I were single. That doesn't sound very convincing, does it? Well, I don't know what else to tell you. It's really hard to explain. It's not something I can put my finger on. Something was missing from my life and I knew it; that's all.

I started to realize that I loved my husband in the same way that I loved my brother. And when I say that I loved my ex-husband, I mean it; I honestly loved him. If you're wondering if it was a physical thing, I can tell you that that wasn't the problem. It was *not* a matter of looks because my first husband was a really good-looking guy. It was just something else.

To give you some background, I really had a fairy tale life. My first husband and his family were very wealthy. Even back in high school when we started dating, he'd buy me diamond jewelry. He bought me a brand new car for my nineteenth birthday. For my twenty-first birthday, he got me a brand new Corvette convertible.

It was a few months after I turned 21 that we got married. After our honeymoon in Hawaii, we moved into our waterfront home. We had our own dock and a beautiful boat, too. We had all of the material things that you could want and then some. Although I didn't need to work, I wanted to, so I worked part-time.

Despite all of the material things, something important was missing. I used to look at my house, my car, and my jewelry and ask myself, "Eve, why aren't you happy?" Every day, I used to walk down our dock and look out at the water, trying to figure out what to do.

The local kids used to swim near there, and they would always wave to me. Sound carries out on the water, and I used to hear them say things to each other about how lucky I was to have all of that money, to have everything a person could ever want. It was really weird to hear that because I didn't *feel* lucky.

I wrestled with my doubts for about a year before it became clear to me that I had to do something. Despite the diamonds, the cars, and the waterfront house, I decided to divorce my first husband. My girlfriends, all of whom thought I was crazy, drove over as soon as they heard the news. I stood in the driveway with them and let them all gang up on me.

While pointing to my house and my car, they kept saying, "Jerry treats you like a princess. He gives you *everything*. *What are you doing*?" I told them that maybe I didn't know what I was doing, but I knew that there had to be something more for me out there. There *had* to be.

It was rough getting back out into the social scene. After 18 months of dating different guys, I met my new husband. I saw him at a club one night out on the dance floor. I said to my girlfriend, "You see that guy? I'm going to marry him." Nine months later, we were married.

About a year after we were married, we went to live in my mother-in-law's house. We were just starting out and money was tight. The three of us—me, my husband, and our newborn son—were packed into my husband's old bedroom.

It had been about three years since I walked away from my first husband and the expensive lifestyle he gave me. My new life had no new cars or water views, but it didn't matter. I was extremely happy. I had finally found out what love was.

There is only one happiness in life,
to love and be loved.

George Sand (1804–1876)
French novelist

She liked me
(Dennis, massage therapist, 48)

It usually cracks people up when I tell them this, but my dad used to say to me, "Denny, you aren't that pretty, so you'd better work on your personality." Hey, I don't blame him. It was true. I never was Mr. Handsome. I was always a chubby guy. Not super fat or anything, but chubby.

In high school, my reputation around town was "the nice young man." I was a wrestler and a football player, but at the same time, I was sort of the gentle giant. All of the girls thought of me as their friend, their buddy. That put me in a position to hear all the girls complain about how bad their boyfriends treated them. I learned *a lot* about women from those conversations.

Even though I never had a girlfriend, there were always a couple of girls in my life. There was a girl I played tennis with and a girl I rode my motorcycle with, but that was only because *they* asked. They had to come to me. I never put the moves on *any* girl because I was too afraid of rejection. I had absolutely no self-confidence.

So that's the way my social life went until I was about 22. That was right around when my life began to take shape. At that age, I was the new owner of a condominium, and I had just been accepted to be an Ohio State trooper.

I was out jogging one day, to get in shape for the upcoming academy training, and I ran into this girl, Tara, I had known in high school. We talked for a few minutes. She said she was back in town and that she was newly divorced. I told her about my new condo, my upcoming state trooper job, and a few other things.

I didn't know it at the time, but she was on the rebound. I was so inexperienced with women that I didn't even know what a rebound *was*. By talking about my condo and my job, I thought that I was just making conversation, but she was sizing me up. She was reading me like a book. She took a quick look at me and she saw security.

Within *four days*, she told me that she loved me and that I was the one for her. Six months later, we were married. The bottom line is that I married the first girl who said she liked me.

The rest of the story is pretty standard stuff. Everything was all about her. One night, back when I was still on the job, a traffic stop went bad and I took one in the chest. Four hours of surgery, three days fighting for my life, fourteen days in the ICU, and she was upset about how the whole thing was affecting *her* life. Apparently, getting shot really inconveniences your spouse. Who knew?

We stayed married for 15 years, but that was only because I didn't want to run out on our daughter. I even overlooked the first two of my wife's three affairs, but when number three rolled around, I was done. I walked out. Hey, I'm a slow learner.

I remarried a few years ago. My beautiful bride and I knew each other for years before we got together. We became good friends first and then just let the rest happen.

Do I regret getting married the first time? Yeah, but what would have stopped me back then? Could I have given that chubby kid any advice? Would he have even taken it?

It was living a lot of years as an adult that showed me that women liked me for who I was. They thought I was funny. Some of the ladies even thought that the whole "teddy bear" thing was kind of sexy, you know? Hey, it takes all kinds.

If I could talk to that chubby kid I'd say, "Hey, hang in there big guy. You're funny. You've got it going on. Take your time and find out who really likes you for who you are."

 Barefoot in Toronto
(Chantal, sales rep, 28)

For six years, I had a lousy relationship with my ex-boyfriend.

He was a *chronic* cheater. Whatever happened, I always looked the other way. I thought I could change him. If I just worked harder at it, I could be the perfect girlfriend and then he wouldn't need those other girls.

The last straw came late one summer night while he and I were sitting in my basement watching TV. The doorbell rang and I went upstairs to get it. There at my door was a beautiful Asian girl who asked if she could speak to *her* boyfriend. I told her that she must be mistaken because there was no one here except me and *my* boyfriend. She called me a bitch and said that her boyfriend's car was parked in my driveway. That's all I needed to hear. I invited her in to confront that bastard.

I went down those basement stairs like a bullet, but he was gone. He had overheard our conversation and, rather than face the two of us, he took off through one of my basement windows. What a weasel.

When I went upstairs and told this other girl what happened, she invited me out to her car so we could go looking for him. What a ride *that* was. We drove all over looking for that sneaky bastard. The funniest thing about it was that he didn't have any shoes on. He was out there somewhere, running around my old neighborhood in Toronto *barefoot*.

I learned a lot during that car ride. I found out that she and I had been given identical cards on all of the holidays and that last Christmas we even got the same gift. I mean that *literally*. He gave me an expensive designer watch on Christmas Eve, but immediately took it back to "get it adjusted." Strangely enough, I never saw it again. He gave her *my* watch on Christmas morning.

At around 3 or 4 A.M. we finally caught up with him. Right there in the road, the three of us hashed it out. We confronted him together because we wanted to make sure that he couldn't play one of us off of the other by telling us different stories. Even though I had gone into it feeling strong, the whole thing ended with me sitting on the curb with my face in my hands, sobbing like a little kid.

I went home and cried for three days. My problem at that point was that I was scared to be single. Would I ever be in another relationship or was I now doomed to be alone? Out of my own weakness, I actually wanted him to call me and tell me that he was wrong, that he was going to stay with me, and that he'd like another chance.

That's when I knew how low I had sunk. After all that, I *still* wanted him? It was a major wake-up call and I knew that hitting the snooze button would only postpone the inevitable. I had to be stronger and turn off the alarm clock and face the day ahead of me.

After those three days were up, I saw an ad in one of the Toronto papers for a telephone dating service. For whatever reason, I gave it a try. Even though my friends thought I was crazy, I had a *blast*.

On average, I was meeting a new guy every other day. None of those dates led to anything, but what they *did* do was to renew my self-esteem. When I think about it now, it's kind of sad that I felt I needed the attention of those guys to feel good about myself again. I always pitied women who were like that, but at time, it made being single less scary.

I still didn't know what I was looking for, but dating all those men sure pointed out what I *didn't* want. That seemed like a good place to start. I had to re-evaluate what I was looking for in a man because obviously my previous standards were *garbage*.

After about a month and a half, I met someone that I ended up seeing exclusively for two months. While I was dating him, I came to a weird realization about myself: I was always attracted to men who weren't that interested in me. The *chase* was the attraction. If they were interested in me, then I was *less* interested in them. So, there I was, in a relationship with this great guy who was totally falling for me, and I was getting bored. I dumped him.

I went back to the telephone dating service and ended up meeting someone else. This time, since he had just broken off his engagement, he wasn't interested in a relationship. Of course, this made me crazy about him. We had a very intense "no strings attached" sexual relationship. It was amazing, but the entire time, I wanted something more.

I was getting into the same routine I had been in before, but this time, I was fully aware of it. At least this guy was actually a really good catch. I was determined not to let myself fall back into that pattern of unrequited love and mental abuse. I decided that I needed some distance from him to just shake things up a bit. I had planned to go look at grad schools, so off I went to the States for about a month.

It was on this trip that I finally got comfortable being single. I accepted the fact that it could be a long time before I found the right person. I also realized that settling for anything less than what I wanted was just a waste of time. I was worthy of someone great; someone who would love me just as much as I loved him. No more pursuing men who weren't interested in me other than perhaps to fool around.

I promised myself that the next man I would be sexually involved with would be the man I would marry. It was a crazy self-imposed restriction, but setting those boundaries helped me focus on finding the right person. Little did I know that it would take me two years to find him.

Those were probably the loneliest, and dare I say, the most sexually frustrating two years of my life. Whenever I went out socializing, I always found myself being the third wheel, surrounded by friends who were all in relationships. Despite those awkward moments, my strength and my independence grew. Ultimately, that new strength made me more attractive.

Finally, towards the end of my first year of school in the U.S., I met the man who would eventually be my husband. We got together through the Internet personals. We wrote long and detailed letters back and forth, both awed by the fact that each of us had not met anyone else with the same level of loyalty, devotion, and caring. We corresponded for three months before we ever met. We exchanged photos, but decided not to speak until our first meeting.

When I got off of that airplane in New York I was nervous, but as soon as I saw him I felt a wave of relief come over me. I always thought that people were crazy who said, "When you find the right one, you'll just know," but I knew right then that he was quite possibly my future husband. Within a few weeks, we were practically living together.

Six months later he came to visit me while I was working in Cannes, France. One day when he took me hiking in the Alps, he dropped down on one knee and proposed to me on top of a mountain. When I finished school a year later, we got married and moved back here to Toronto. That was about five years ago.

I'm glad that I did what I did. I didn't give up. I didn't settle.

I acknowledged that all men were not the same and that eventually I would find love, and the man that was right for me. I just never realized that love could be as wonderful as it is now with my husband. It's really stuff I only thought existed in stories, TV, and movies, but it really can happen.

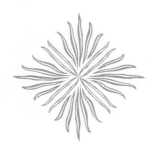

Money and Finance

Ordinary riches can be stolen.
Real riches cannot.

Oscar Wilde (1854–1900)
Irish author and poet

My money

There have been times in my life when I didn't have any money, and times when I did. As things move along and different events unfold, I'm not sure if the next phase of my life will include any money or not. Strangely enough, now that I'm approaching this time of personal financial uncertainty, I've never been looser with my spending. Not reckless, mind you, but certainly less inhibited than I've ever been. I tell myself that if Rome is going to burn, I might as well fiddle.

Many of us have regrets when it comes to money, but I wanted to hear something from those I interviewed other than the obvious or easy answers. What did they know about money? How did they learn it? What *didn't* they know that ended up hurting them? What, if anything, did they wish they could have done differently?

Guitars and amps and crap
(Chris, small business owner, 40)

Right after high school, I was still living at home with my parents. I wasn't going to college, so I had a full-time job. I don't remember what I earned, but I had no expenses back then so whatever it was, it was a *fortune*.

I took all of the money I made and blew it on drugs and *a lot* of guitars. I literally spent *thousands* of dollars on guitars and amps and crap. It was ridiculous.

I bought stuff I never even used, guitars I never even *played*. There were a few of them that I saw in the music store and brought home just because they looked cool. I'd just set them up on a guitar stand in the corner and that was it. Years later, I ended up selling all of that stuff at a huge loss.

My needs were so small back then that I could have saved a small fortune to put down on my first house. If I had done that, I'd be ready now to step up to a bigger house. A lot of people my age are doing that, but I can't. I'm still on step one.

Whenever I feel like torturing myself, I think about all of the money I wasted. If I had just saved it for a house, that would've been great, but if I had *invested* the money, it would be worth a fortune now. I once calculated that if, 20 years ago, I had put that cash in a few aggressive stocks, it would be worth almost six million dollars today. Yeah, it's easy for me to cherry pick the stocks now, but even if my estimate is only 10% accurate, that's still nearly $600,000. Yeah, I could have also lost a lot of it too, but I lost *all* of it by blowing it on coke and crap.

Out of pocket
(Todd, customer service agent, 57)

I was 25 years old when I came back from Vietnam. It was 1972, my wife and I were newly married, and we had just bought a house. We considered ourselves to be planners, so we started thinking about our financial future.

Back then, anyone in the service could join this savings and investment plan. I can't remember what it was called, but the plan was a combination of three things: insurance, investments, and savings. We heard a few good things about it, so my wife and I called them and set up an appointment. This guy came over and met with us for about an hour. He asked us what our goals were, what our plans were for the future, and then he had us set up sort of a dream sheet.

We told the guy that we wanted to pay off our house, retire in comfort, and put the two kids that we didn't even *have* yet through college. He took lots of notes and then said that he'd be back in two weeks to make a presentation of his ideas.

Two weeks later, the guy came back and showed me and my wife how we could do everything that we wanted to do. It wasn't just his opinion, and it wasn't wishful thinking either. *He had everything figured out to the last dollar.*

He knew I was going to put a total of 20 years in the service. He knew what my income would be as the years went by, making conservative guesses about when I'd get promoted. If we put about $100 a month into this investment setup, over time, we would be able to achieve *all* of our goals. I'd also have to put half of any raises I got into the plan too. We liked what we heard, so we signed up that night.

We contributed to the plan for a year. At the end of that first year, there was a window where the money was still ours to withdraw if we wanted to. By that time, my wife was pregnant and we wanted to furnish the house. We could have cut down on our expenses, bought cheaper furniture, or we could have just waited till we had the money to buy the stuff we wanted, but we didn't. We took all of that money out of the plan and stopped investing all together.

We ended up falling into the trap that a lot of people do. We ran up a lot of credit card debt buying things that we could have waited to buy. Every month, I ended up making the minimum payment on a few credit cards that I had maxed out. The *interest* I paid every month was equal to the amount that I could have been putting in my investment plan. That's the real shame of it.

I got so caught up in paying the bills that I forgot to pay myself first. Even though I had heard that expression "pay yourself first" before, I didn't understand the importance of it till after the fact. I didn't even start saving again for 18 years. It was only after I got out of the service and was looking at paying college tuition for my daughter that I changed my ways. I was 43 then. I missed 18 years of investing, 18 years of compounding.

Let me tell you, it was tough trying to pay my daughter's tuition out of pocket. She didn't even go to a really expensive private school; she went to a state school. In order to manage, my wife and I had to do some things we didn't want to do. That's the thing nobody tells you. You're going to pay either way, so you might as well pay early on when you don't have to pay as much. Putting it off only makes it worse; putting it off costs more.

If I had followed that investment plan from day one, I could have retired after my 20 years in the service. The house would have been paid off and we'd have my pension and the investment money to live off of. As it was, I had to get a job after I got out.

A good friend of mine joined the plan back when I did, but he stayed with it. He retired a millionaire.

> *It is not the knowing that is*
> *difficult, but the doing.*
>
> Chinese proverb

 ## Know money, or no money
(Reggie, sanitation worker, 47)

Ever since I was a kid, I made money. I've always worked and I've always had money, but back then I never knew what to do with it. I didn't have a plan. I blew *all* my cash as a young guy.

My dad used to say, "Save your money," but he never said anything else. He never said that he was saving *his* money. If he had talked about *why* I should save my money, maybe the message would have sunk in. The one thing I can remember my dad saying about money was, "It's not what you make, it's what you spend that counts." I absolutely believe that.

My parents never talked about money in front of us as kids. We were sort of kept in the dark when it came to financial concerns. We never heard them talk about taxes, bills, or the mortgage—none of that stuff. I don't mean that they should have scared us by talking about the unpaid bills or anything, we just never heard about the role that money had in a normal household. Because of that, I had no idea about how money worked or what you really needed it for.

Before you think I'm crazy, think about this: If you never told a kid about how water got to your house or where it came from, they would think that water just magically appeared every time they turned on the faucet. The same thing goes for electricity and the wall switch. One way or the other, kids have to be taught about *everything*. I know it would have helped me to have some understanding of money as a kid.

What I tell my son about money is exactly what I wish somebody would have told me. I tell him to save half and blow the other half. This way, he's got the best of both worlds. He's got a plan. There's no guilt either. He can save for important things like college, a car, a house; whatever. And he can also enjoy himself with his friends. He can do all of the stupid things kids love to do with their money. It's not a perfect plan, but it lets him save and lets him be a kid and enjoy himself.

When you think about it, that's what really catches up with people: the fact that they didn't have a plan. People just end up somewhere doing something. And that "something" usually isn't what they wanted. That applies to money just as much as it does to anything else.

Now that everybody I know has a house and a wife and kids, they all wish that they were in a better place in life, financially speaking.

They all say things that start off like this: "I probably should have . . ." You can fill in the blank with anything like, "stayed in school," "gotten my degree," or "planned ahead." Those are the ones I hear a lot.

Some people are able to see this sort of thing early on. Some people just seem to know what they're going to need and they stay focused. Those are the people who get established. Those are the people who succeed.

I try to tell the 18-year-old kids I work with about this sort of stuff. I tell them that it's important to save and to plan, but they're 18 years old. They think they're going to live forever. They don't listen to an old guy like me.

 ## Crazy money
(Chantal, sales rep, 28)

My bum of an ex-boyfriend needed money to start up a landscaping business. He had no credit history, but because I was a college student with a part-time job, *I* was eligible to borrow up to $8,000. Yup, I gave him $8,000.

When I gave him that money, I knew I shouldn't have done it. I was ignoring my instincts, but I wanted to impress upon him what a good girlfriend I was. Can you believe it? Why didn't somebody just shoot me?

We broke up a few months later, and I knew there was absolutely no way that loser was ever going to pay me back. Things were okay for a while because as long as I was still in school, no one expected me to start making loan payments. When I finished school, they came looking for me. *That's* when I was in a jam.

I was still pretty young back then. I had no job, no way of making good on that debt. I began defaulting on the payments. I'm not proud of it, but I ran away from it. I left my home town in Canada and came to the U.S. to begin a graduate study program.

While I was doing my second graduate degree in the States, I saw an ad for an available scholarship. This was the *only* scholarship available to Canadian students, so on a whim, I applied for it. It consisted of $10,000 in cash and another $30,000 worth of spending money and expenses for a six-week wine tour in California, Italy, and France. Luckily, I got it.

My tuition in the States was being covered by my parents, so the $10,000 was mine to spend however I chose. Because of the favorable exchange rate between the U.S. and the Canadian dollar, I was able to pay off the rest of my debt and still had about half of it left to spend however I wanted. It was just luck, fate, God, or who knows what that saved me from that stupid mistake.

What's the moral of my story? Is it that you should duck your financial responsibilities, flee the country, and hope to win a scholarship? Maybe, but for me, the moral of the story is you shouldn't lend money to bums. Hell, you shouldn't date them either.

Cash or charge?
(John, attorney, 48)

After college, I had worked for several years in a supermarket, saving my money and living with my parents. This strategy allowed me to amass quite a bit of cash. My goal was to save enough to pay my own way through law school.

I always considered myself to be a smart guy. Good grades, hard work, saving money—all of these things came easily to me. But I never realized how little I knew about money. It took a really stupid mistake to show me just how financially ignorant I was.

When I went to law school, I was able to pay for all but the last semester in cash. When the time came to decide how I would pay for the last semester, I literally had no idea what it meant to borrow money.

I looked at the situation and saw that I had two choices: borrow the money via a student loan or use one of my credit cards. Regardless of how foolish it sounds, I viewed those two options as being the same. Now, of course, I know that they are two completely different choices.

A student loan might be simply described as "straight" debt. You borrow X amount at a certain rate of interest and you slowly pay it off. The amount never gets bigger. Credit card debt might be described as "compounding" debt. The difference between these two choices is huge.

Yes, the credit card company loans you the money at a certain rate of interest, but if you're not able to make monthly payments that exceed the amount of interest accrued, then that interest becomes part of what you owe and then they start charging you interest on the interest. In this situation, the amount can and usually does get bigger.

To put it simply, if you borrow money from the bank, you *always* know how much you owe them. If you borrow money from a credit card, you've got to watch it. You can easily end up on the hook for a lot more than you bargained for.

That one mistake, made because of my naiveté and ignorance about money, ended up costing me a few thousand dollars. It's really important to learn how money works and grows. If you don't know how money works, then you will always be at the mercy of those who do.

 Bet your bottom dollar
(Matthew, stockbroker, 38)

The one experience that taught me the most about money happened years ago. I was 24 years old and living in Boston. Although I had graduated from college two years earlier, I wasn't making use of my degree. I was spinning my wheels working in a supermarket.

Like a lot of people, I was living paycheck to paycheck. My bachelor lifestyle made it easy to be a bit irresponsible with money. Blame it on youth, blame it on inexperience, but that's the way I was back then.

This one time, I had worked my budget so tight, I knew I had just enough money to last until my next paycheck. All I had to do was to hang on for a week. My gas tank was full, the bills were paid; all I needed was to buy food to last me for the week. I took the small amount of cash that I had and went down to the food store.

As carefully as I could, I weighed the importance of every item I picked up off the shelves. I did the math in my head, keeping track of the grand total as I went down each aisle. It was not a comfortable feeling.

The guy working the register gave me a funny look as I put my items down in front of him. Maybe he noticed how nervous I was. I remember thinking, "What if I don't have enough? What am I going to put back? *Put back*?! I need *all* of this stuff!"

My items were totaled up and the amount due showed in the digital display window on the cash register. I handed the guy my money and he handed me my change. He handed me back $1.03.

I quickly pocketed the three cents, but I held that dollar bill in my hand for a minute. I just sort of stared at it for a moment or two. You know that expression, "Bet your bottom dollar"? Well, I was looking at my bottom dollar, my *last* dollar in the whole world! So what did I do? I spent it on gum.

As I walked out of that store I kept saying to myself, "I spent my bottom dollar. I spent my *bottom dollar*." It was a weird feeling.

It felt a little crazy and a little reckless to mismanage my money like that, but maybe that's why I allowed it to happen. Maybe it made me feel wild and rebellious or something; I don't know. What I *do* know is that halfway through that next week I was going out of my mind! I had absolutely no money, *nothing*. I was scared to death that something would happen: a flat tire, an emergency, something. What if I met a nice girl? What if I needed to mail a letter? The three cents I had wouldn't even buy a postcard stamp.

Lucky for me, I managed to get through the rest of the week without incident, but I never did anything like that again. In fact, I've sort of moved in the other direction. Now I try to save and invest as much of my money as possible. No more bottom dollar.

# Today
(Samantha, educational administrator, 63)

The best thing my husband and I ever did was spend our money on travel. When his business took off, we used the extra money to take one dream vacation after another. I had always worked too, which was good, so my money was spent on landscaping and redecorating.

For the past 25 years, we've really seen the world, or at least the places we wanted to see. We've been on all different kinds of trips: ski trips, island trips, city trips, etc. Every one of those places offered something different and we really loved them all.

The knowledge and experience that travel brings broadens you as a person. You can expose yourself and your children to so much through travel. You see other worlds, other perspectives. It changes you in ways that other experiences can't. It enriches you in ways that you simply cannot duplicate by any other means.

Almost every day, my husband and I sit and talk about some of our favorite trips. We ask each other about the things that made this or that trip so special. You'd think that we'd get tired of talking about it, but we don't.

Possessions come and go. Whatever you buy, someone or something can always take it away from you. No one can ever take experiences away from you. No one can ever take the thrill out of your heart the first time you step to the edge of the Grand Canyon or walk into the Coliseum in Rome. No one can ever repossess the smiles on your kids' faces when they see the color of the water surrounding an exotic island.

Recently, my husband's health has worsened and it doesn't allow us to travel the way we used to. It's for that reason that I'm grateful for having gone when we had the chance. We certainly couldn't take those trips now. Had we waited, we would have missed out on all of those spectacular experiences.

The idea of waiting, putting off your life while waiting for something else to happen, always struck me as stupid. Yes, we could have saved all of that money that we spent on vacations, but for what? My husband and I know many couples who are compulsive savers. After so many years, they're not savers, they're hoarders. They don't even know what money *is* anymore.

> *Tomorrow do thy worst,*
> *for I have lived today.*
>
> John Dryden (1631–1700)
> English poet

The richest man in the graveyard

In the three years or so that I worked in my father's insurance office, I got the chance to meet a great many people. Most of them were friendly, several of them were rude, and a few of them were wonderfully eccentric. It was a good opportunity to see what it was like to work with the public.

One of my father's best customers was an elderly gentleman named Jerry Taylor. Mr. Taylor owned many nice houses and insured them through my father's office. Roughly every ten months, Mr. Taylor would come in and insure another house, as he added to his growing real estate portfolio. Because he was still expanding his real estate holdings when I left that job, I have no idea how many houses he actually ended up owning.

During his visits to the office, Mr. Taylor was always polite, respectful, and extremely courteous. He never made a late payment and never had a cross word with anyone. He was the perfect customer.

One day after work, Mr. Taylor's name came up as my father and I sat around the office talking. We both admired him for the way he carried himself and for the way that he treated others. I commented on his amazing real estate holdings and wondered what he did with all of that money. My father said something like, "Jim, I don't think he really has any money." The shocked look on my face told my father that I needed a bit of an explanation.

Because my dad had known Mr. Taylor for years, he knew things about him that I didn't. My father said, "Jim, you know that I think Mr. Taylor is a terrific guy, right? Well, I want you to ask him a few things the next time you see him. When he comes in to pay his bill, I want you to notice a few things about him. Things you might not have noticed before." My father mentioned the things he wanted me to ask and the things he wanted me to notice. After that, we let the matter drop.

About two months later, I saw Mr. Taylor again. He sat down at my desk and as I reviewed some of his information, I casually began to ask him some of the questions that my father had mentioned. The answers that he gave changed everything I thought I knew about him.

As I reviewed his file, I asked him if he had taken any vacations lately. He replied by politely saying that he would never spend money on something as frivolous as a trip. We talked about hobbies, interests, recreation—anything and everything I could think of. Each time that Mr. Taylor would reply, he'd say something about not wanting to spend any money. This pattern continued throughout our conversation.

Another thing my father had wanted me to notice was how Mr. Taylor was dressed. I had never noticed it before, but the shirt he was wearing had several stains on it. They were not the type of stains that you would have if you had just spent the day painting the garage; they were older than that. They were faded. They looked as if they had seen many days and a lot of trips through the washing machine.

When he got up to leave, I saw that his pants were in the same condition as his shirt. In addition to a stain or two, there was a hole at the knee. There was also a small hole in the elbow of his jacket. I walked Mr. Taylor out to the parking lot and I watched him drive away in his rusty old '62 Impala.

Before you judge me too harshly, please understand that my opinion of a person has nothing to do with the car they drive or the condition of their clothing. My opinion of Mr. Taylor could not have been higher. He was a gentleman in every sense of the word. My father wanted me to notice these things only because I had made such a big deal about Mr. Taylor's money.

My father and I knew the value of Mr. Taylor's properties and we also knew that only two or three of them still had mortgages. Since he rented all of his properties, except the 49-year-old home in which he lived, we also knew that he earned a large sum of money every month from rental income. Surely that money went somewhere.

Because we also insured all of his adult children, their spouses, and all of his grandchildren, we knew that the family was in good health. We knew that they all had good jobs and healthy financial statements as well. So where was all of that money going? The answer was that it went nowhere. It was spent on nothing. It was spent on no one.

Despite the fact that, in the late 1980s, Mr. Taylor's real estate portfolio was probably worth over $900,000, he looked and acted like a man who lived at the poverty line. It is certainly an honorable and respectable thing to work hard, to be careful, and to save money. No one doubts that, but where is the balance? Where are the rewards?

It bothered me to see Mr. Taylor in this new way. I didn't want to see that hard-working old man wearing a stained shirt and ripped pants. I didn't want to see him driving away in a rusty old car.

The saddest thing about this story is that all Mr. Taylor was doing was carrying money for someone else. The only people who will ever enjoy it will be his grandchildren and the IRS. Mr. Taylor made himself into a courier. As long as he lives, he's just carrying money into the future for someone else.

What value does money have if it is never spent? If Mr. Taylor spent his nights staring at his financial statements and marveling at the huge numbers, what's the difference between him and a child who scribbles a fake check for a zillion dollars? Both are just numbers and words on paper. Money is just an idea until you use it; *then* it becomes real.

Because it was none of my business, I never asked Mr. Taylor why he did what he did. If I had asked him why he didn't spend any money, I'm sure he would have told me that he was waiting for something. He would have talked about some goal or some final dollar amount, but no matter what it was, I know that he would have never reached it.

Since that day, I've always looked for people like Mr. Taylor. If you look, you will see them everywhere. They are people who have money, but deny themselves everything. If asked, I'm sure they would tell you that they are only waiting until they retire or until their kids move out or until . . . *Then* they'll enjoy themselves, they would tell you. *Then* they'll live.

These people, having lived their entire lives clutching their money to their chests, cannot change. In their hearts, they never cross the finish line; therefore, they never let go.

To this day, if I talk about someone who has money but never spends any of it, I say that they've got "Jerry Taylor money."

A wise man should have money
in his head, but not in his heart.

Jonathan Swift (1667–1745)
Irish writer and satirist

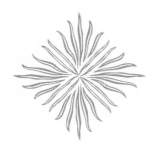

Looking Back

WHISPERS OF HIGH SCHOOL, COLLEGE, AND THE ARMED SERVICES

In youth we learn; in age we understand.

Marie von Ebner-Eschenbach (1830–1916)
German novelist

Purely by accident

L ast summer, I was coming home from a restaurant with an old friend. We were driving along in his Porsche 911 SC4. It was a bit strange for me to look over and see him behind the wheel of such an amazing car. After all, I had known him when we were just a couple of stupid kids, driving around most of the night in his beat-up '68 AMC Rebel. The "gray ghost," as we used to call it. We had come a long way since then.

We began congratulating each other, telling each other how far we'd come and how we seemed to do "it" better than the next guy. Despite all of the self-congratulatory talk that took place in that Porsche, something about it didn't seem quite right. It felt as if we were overlooking something important in our haste to give each other the "Man of the Year" award.

He and I had always been pretty smart growing up, but back in high school we were both underachievers. Either one of us could have been easily classified as one of the weird or unusual kids. We, like many others, wandered through our youth without goals and without plans. We got nondescript college degrees and spun our wheels after graduation in dead end jobs. What, if anything, did we do that was so special?

After giving it some thought, it occurred to me that in our case, it was not so much what we *did*, but what we *avoided* doing that mattered. Yes, we were underachievers, but unintentionally we did some of the most important things that a person who lacks direction can do:

- We did not stop moving forward. We pursued an education.

- We stayed out of trouble. We avoided incarceration, and unwanted pregnancies. (Theirs, *not* ours!)

- We avoided big mistakes. We managed not to damage our bodies through accidents, drug abuse, or recklessness.

- We did not allow irrational fears to hold us back. We were not afraid to embrace unique opportunities. (This only became true for us towards the end of our time in college.)

The things mentioned above might seem overly simplistic, but they undoubtedly played a large part in our success. Even though we didn't know it at the time, we kept our options open. We were preparing ourselves for opportunity so that when we *did* mature, when we *did* find some focus, we could capitalize on any situation.

Purely by accident, that is what I began to do while I was still in high school. When most of my classmates were making college plans, I was trying to convince my parents that I didn't need an education. It's not as if I had anything against college, it's just that I saw it as something I wasn't going to need. My passion was music. I was a singer and a songwriter.

Luckily for me, my parents always encouraged my interest in a musical career, but they also instilled in me the importance of getting a college degree. I listened to them and it turned out to be some of the best advice I've ever gotten because although I went on to pursue both goals simultaneously, it was my education that proved to have the most value. Years later, I was reminded of the importance of that good advice.

I can still remember the two Southern gentlemen who interviewed

me for my big airline job. They sat behind their big oak desks and chuckled at my B.A. in English. They had been interviewing thousands of applicants with degrees in mechanical engineering, aerospace technology, and dozens of other technical fields. I might as well have been sitting there with a degree in basket-weaving.

Regardless of what they might have thought of my degree, they hired me. The requirement was not that applicants have a degree in the field of aviation. The requirement was not even for a degree in the sciences. The requirement was for a degree, *any* degree.

When I was 18 years old and trying to decide whether or not I should go to college, I had no idea that 15 years later, my career plans would hinge on whether or not I had a college diploma. The fact that I had the degree and therefore got the job is not proof of my genius or my ability to read the tea leaves. It simply means that I was willing to do something, to complete college, without knowing how it might benefit me at the time. I did not turn my back on my musical interests; I simply added something else to my life.

This chapter focuses on my interviewees' responses to my questions about their formal education. It might seem as if I'm placing undue importance on education, but this is simply what my interviews revealed. When it comes to the choices that the young can make that will help them later in life, this one is at the top of the list.

Although there are certainly other choices besides education, I'm guessing that those I interviewed favored this one because, for most people, it's the most obvious and readily available choice. Other chapters in this book deal with adventure, discovery, practical knowledge, and personal growth. *All* of those things can help us to grow and develop as people.

An interesting aside to all of this is that almost every one of those I interviewed expressed some degree of regret when it came to their education. Most of their comments weren't flashy, dramatic, or even quotable, but I found their consistency and their sheer numbers to be unavoidable. Seeing as how most of their comments weren't broad enough or weren't in the form of a story, I could not find a way to include them here in a meaningful way. Simply typing "I wish I had tried harder in school" or "I should have gotten a degree" several hundred times would not mean much to anyone. Only interviewees who told me a story about their experiences have been included.

Perhaps the most interesting thing about this particular topic is that not a single one of the people I interviewed ever said that their time spent getting an education was wasted. Not one.

Having an education is like carrying a key. It weighs nothing but can open doors for us that might have otherwise remained closed. It doesn't matter if we ever use it. It will always there for us, just in case.

Learning is a treasure that will
follow its owner everywhere.

Chinese proverb

 # Nobody gets into Stanford
(Alicia, management consultant, 34)

Right at the beginning of my senior year, I started applying to colleges. My sights were set on Stanford. It was my dream school. It was only about two hours from my house, and with its beautiful campus and excellent reputation, it seemed like the perfect place for me. My back-up choices were some schools in the UC system: UCLA, UC Santa Barbara, and UC Santa Cruz.

The application process involved different things for different schools, but most of them had application fees. Those fees kept me kind of cautious. I didn't have a lot of money to throw around, so I didn't want to send any applications to schools where I didn't think I'd get in.

One of Stanford's requirements was for me to get a recommendation letter from one of my teachers. Since my student advisor was also my advanced Spanish teacher, I figured that I could meet with her, get her to advise me, and then ask her to write a letter for me too. I wasn't particularly fond of her, but I chose her as my advisor because she was the most advanced Spanish teacher in the school. Something about her was a little off, but I thought that she'd be the best person to advise me because I had just gotten back from a summer semester in Spain and I figured that she'd see me as an equal. Maybe she'd think that I was pretty worldly for a high school student.

I wasn't nervous at all about the meeting with her. I was ranked number two in my class, I had great SAT scores, and because of the advanced placement courses that I took, my GPA was a 4.2.

I hoped that she'd be a little impressed, and she'd just help me to do what I needed to do to get into Stanford. That's all.

Our meeting began right on time. I sat down where I was supposed to, at a table at the far end of the room. My advisor was there, but she never sat down. She just kept pacing around the room, moving papers around and removing bulletins that were posted on the walls. She said a few words to me over her shoulder, but she never even looked at me. I started talking about my college plans, but she didn't say anything. When I mentioned Stanford, she *still* didn't say anything. I mentioned it again and asked her what she thought my chances were of getting in. I was looking for a little support, a little cheerleading.

Without even looking up from her paperwork she said, "Oh, don't even bother. Nobody gets into Stanford." And just like that, it was over. What I thought was going to be a thirty-minute strategy session turned into a two-sentence dismissal of my dream.

The idea that I got from her was that I wasn't good enough for Stanford; I wasn't worthy. I walked out of that meeting feeling completely disillusioned. I never even applied to Stanford.

The idea that I was somehow unworthy stayed with me. It really impacted my performance when I went to UCSB the following year. I stopped trying so hard. I found myself saying, "If I worked this hard and still couldn't get where I wanted to go, why should I even bother?" My grades began to suffer. So much so that I wasn't able to get into this UCLA Ph.D. program in which I later became interested. It's funny how the impact of one conversation can spread out through your life.

I regret that I didn't have a strong enough sense of self to bounce back from her comments. I didn't even respect her that much, but I let her knock me off course, and I *stayed* off course. You can't always let other people guide you. You need to listen and take in all information as input, but you've got to filter it. I let some woman, who I did even have a high regard for, talk me out of my dream. That's *my* fault, not hers.

My husband and I live in Santa Barbara. We go to a lot of business meetings and parties where we run into Stanford graduates. I never say anything, but my husband always asks the Stanford grads how they got in, what their transcripts were like, the whole thing. When he tells them my story, mentions my GPA, my SAT scores, and my extra-curricular activities, they all look at the floor and shake their heads in disbelief. They all say, "Oh yeah. She *definitely* would have gotten in."

 # The role of the airhead
(Rana, pharmaceutical research chemist, 25)

Back in high school, I was "Miss Popular." I was a varsity cheerleader, and I was really outgoing, too. Growing up in Orange County, California, surrounded by all of those blondes, my dark hair and Mediterranean features got a lot of attention. I took full advantage of the interest the guys showed me. Life was great.

My parents worked long hours and they didn't really watch over me that closely. I drank a lot, and I did a lot of drugs too. I was a fair student, but I could have been much better. Whatever grades I got, I got them without studying. I did a lot more beach work than school work, if you know what I mean.

Early in my junior year, Mr. Post, my chemistry teacher, asked me if I would volunteer to be one of his assistants. Teacher's assistants are expected to help grade papers, organize certain things, and to sort of act as academic examples to the other students. It seemed like a good idea, so I said yes.

Right off the bat, things didn't go well. I completely flaked out. I was so busy running around with all of the guys I knew that I never even showed up to help Mr. Post. I didn't stick to what I had said I'd do.

He confronted me one day after class. I told him something, but he caught me in a lie. I was busted.

He sat me down and said something that I've never forgotten. He said, "A person's word is who that person is." When I tried to con him some more by playing the role of the airhead, he said, "Look, you've got potential. Why are you putting yourself down like this?"

Everyone in school knew me as a partier and so did Mr. Post. He told me that I owed it to myself to be more than just a social butterfly or someone who got high all the time. He thought I could be a great student if I wanted to be. He said, "The guys who are chasing after you are chasing after ten other girls too. You're not the only beautiful thing out there. When you get older, you're not going to look like you do now. What then? Your mind lasts longer than your looks. Learn to develop your mind."

All of the things Mr. Port said to me were true, but I didn't act on all of them right away. How could I? I just made one or two small changes at first. For starters, I stopped cutting class. That went okay, so I started to make school my first priority. I found out that I could still have boyfriends and a social life, and that was great. I still went to the beach, but only after my work was done. Mr. Post was right when he said, "You can still have fun, but you need to take care of yourself."

Talking to Mr. Post a little every day is what caused me to change.

He was sort of a father figure, and that slow and steady influence is what changed things for me.

Another thing that developed over time was how I saw my friends. Most of them were pretty wild. They weren't really bad, but they weren't the best thing for me either. I kept all of those people as my friends, but I chose who I was going to hang out with a little more carefully after that.

All in all, it took me about a year to straighten out. Not only did I become a better student, but I became a better daughter to my mom. I was more conscientious, more considerate.

After I graduated high school, I got my Bachelor's degree and then went on to graduate from Columbia University with a Master's degree in organic chemistry. Now I'm a pharmaceutical research chemist for one of the most prestigious pharmaceutical companies in the country.

Back in high school, I was like a matchstick. There was some potential energy there, but nothing was ever going to happen as long as I was standing still. I *had* the potential; I just needed a push. Some chemicals, like gasoline or the stuff on the head of a match, have stored energy in them. Once you introduce the ignition source, they burn.

Three letters
(Carol, professor of accounting, 49)

Ever since I was about 16 years old, I wanted to be an accountant. As I got closer to high school graduation, closer to the time to make some decisions about colleges and whatnot, I made an appointment to see the guidance counselor. My high school guidance counselor said that I wasn't college material. I figured he knew best, so *I* decided that I must not be college material. After graduation, I got a job instead of going off to school.

After working for a while, I took one course at night, just to see if

I *still* wasn't college material. It turned out that I could handle it, so a year later I went full-time at my community college. Two years later, I graduated with my Associate's degree.

Even so, I missed out on going away to college, going straight to college after high school. I missed out on all of those "young person" experiences. It was like I was never young. I was always a young adult instead.

Okay, I can blame my guidance counselor for the first part of the story, but this next part is *entirely* my fault. After I got my two-year degree, instead of going on to a four-year school, I decided to get married. I was "in love." I wanted the white picket fence, the whole nine yards.

There's nothing wrong with love and marriage, but you can't lose yourself in it either. I know lots of women who fell in love and got married, but they also kept pursuing their goals. My dream of being an accountant got shelved when I decided to get married.

When my marriage fell apart, I had nothing. Because of where I let someone else steer me and because of what I allowed myself to settle for, I never became a Certified Public Accountant. It's what I could have done and it's what I should have done, but it never happened.

I went on to get my Bachelor's degree and later my Master's degree, but by then I was entrenched in a corporate job, making good money. I didn't feel I had the time to become a CPA. I left that job after a few years, took some teaching courses, and became a professor of accounting.

Even though I've got years of business experience and a few degrees, I don't have those three letters, CPA, and it *haunts* me. A week doesn't go by without someone asking me, "Are you a CPA?" There is *no* acceptance in my field without those three letters.

Keep true to the dreams of thy youth.

Johan Friedrich von Schiller (1759–1805)
German dramatist

I *am* smart
(Jeff, network administrator for the Air National Guard, 38)

Education was not stressed in my house. My dad always used to make fun of college guys. Because he had been in the Air National Guard since he was young, he knew a lot of officers. He felt that many of them were terrible leaders, but they were allowed to be officers because they had college degrees. He used to say that someone who went to college was "an educated ass."

The things that my dad said had an effect on me. Needless to say, he never pushed the idea of school. He dropped out of high school in his senior year.

My dad raised me to be a conservative and all of my teachers in high school were liberal burnouts who dodged the draft. Right off the bat, I couldn't stand most of them. That attitude, coupled with a few other things, really worked against me. You could say that I had a few difficulties when I was in school.

My grades in school were all right: mostly C's and B's. Math was a good subject for me, but English was terrible. I couldn't write or spell to save my life. Every once in a while, I come across something that I wrote when I was in school and I'm shocked at how childish it looks. The handwriting is terrible and every sentence seems to be missing a few words.

The bottom line is that I had no confidence in high school. I wasn't a great student to begin with and when you add my father's influence to the situation, you can see that I was starting from a bad place. Because I had big problems with English, I convinced myself that I wasn't smart.

My poor grades and my general disinterest in school caused me to sign up for special education courses in electronics. The classes focused on radio and television repair. I *loved* them. I finished with an A+, which was the highest grade in the class. It's kind of strange because

I managed to get that grade even though I used to cut out all the time.

My new electronics skills were put to work immediately. I got out of Driver's Ed class by fixing the Driver's Ed teacher's TV. After I fixed the gym teacher's broken digital scale, I never had to go to gym again. Pretty wild, huh?

After I graduated from high school, I joined the Air National Guard and went to their Avionics and Communications school. I worked and studied harder than I had ever done before. The hard work paid off because I aced every test throughout the entire six-month course. I got a perfect score on each one. There were a few sections that I didn't even think I'd pass, but I aced them too.

My success in the Air National Guard gave me a new confidence in myself. It showed me that I was smart. It showed me that academic success is a process, a formula. I just kept following the formula of self-discipline and study and I kept succeeding. It's a shame that I found this out about myself after high school. Had I known these things and felt this way back then, I know I would have done really well.

I wish that I had gone to college. It doesn't make you a better person, it just gives you more opportunities. For example, when I left my own business, I went out looking for a job. Even though my experience and qualifications were great and my interview test scores were higher than most of the other applicants, I found it hard to get hired without a degree. That's not fair, but that's life. That's the game life plays.

My parents didn't push me academically, but I'm not going to make that mistake with my son. My wife and I want our son to feel comfortable in school. I don't want him to feel like he's the idiot in class, like I did.

When I talk to my son about school, I try to do things differently than my father did. We talk about his homework, his grades, and his future. We talk about college a lot too. I stress the importance of education and I push him a bit. I want him to have the chance to go to college if he wants to.

As I said, I'm *trying* to get my son to understand, but so far it's not working. He might have to learn it for himself.

Cute and funny
(Debbie, educational administrator, 35)

I was a social wimp in high school. Looking back, I cared way too much about what other people thought of me. This attitude made me withdraw from the whole social experience. I just didn't participate.

There were so many things offered at my school that I never took advantage of. And it was all free! Music, art, clubs, athletics—you name it and our school had it. But I did none of it. When are you ever going to get the chance again in life to have access to all of this stuff? Free stuff! I wish I had taken up the cello.

Once I got established in college, I made a conscious decision to be more outgoing. I approached this new challenge in a really weird and direct way. One Saturday afternoon, I went around my dorm and asked people this question: "When you first look at me, what word comes to mind?" The number one answer was "cute." *Not* sexy, *not* beautiful, but cute! The number two answer was "funny." So I decided to run with "cute and funny."

"Cute" was great, but there wasn't really much that I could do with that. I guess I just continued to be cute! Because people had given me "funny" as their number two response, I decided that that's where I had some room to work. From then on, I made it my business to be as outgoing and as funny as possible. I thought, *You want funny?! I'll give you funny!*

The whole "survey" thing was great for me. It forced me to be honest with myself, to meet other people, and to really transform. It worked too. I was able to connect with so many more people than before. It worked so well in fact that now I can talk to *anybody*.

Anyway, if I had any advice to give someone, it would be this: It's hard not to worry about what others will think or say about you, but you need to stay out of that trap. The sooner you get out of that rut, the sooner you can get on with life, *your* life.

Also, if you have any interests, explore them now. Do it *now*, while you're young. Sometimes, "later" is too late.

 # Trust
(Dan, computer engineer, 40)

In my house, there was no real emphasis on getting an education. My father quit school in the seventh grade and went to work to help support his family. Because of my dad's history, my brother and I were raised to respect earning rather than learning. Consequently, I never saw the need to apply myself in school. While others were preparing for the SAT's or applying to colleges, I just sort of sat it out. I had other interests.

Due to my dad's influence and my own poor point of view, I was just an average student in high school. I had ideas about certain areas of study that I wanted to pursue, but my parents and the guidance counselors pushed me towards the things *they* thought were best for me. That didn't help the situation much.

Television production was a real interest of mine. Our high school had quite a big media department. They had their own little studio set up behind the library. There was always something being taped or produced in there. With a little direction, maybe I could have made a career of it. One of my biggest regrets is that I listened to what others said instead of listening to my own gut feelings.

Right after high school graduation, I enrolled in a two-year program at a technical school. My area of study was electronics.

The academics were no problem. As I matured, I began to apply myself more, even if I couldn't see a reason to do so. I was an adult and it seemed like the right thing to do.

After I graduated from technical school, I went out looking for my first real job. When I went on my first interview, I was shocked at what I saw. It was like a casting call. There were hundreds of applicants walking up and down the halls and in and out of various rooms. I remember saying to myself, *I've got to compete against all of these people?* It was quite an eye-opening experience. For the first time, I got a taste of what the job market was going to be like.

Within a year of getting my first job, I started to feel a bit uneasy about my educational background. Maybe it was because the guys I worked with were older than me, but whatever the reason, I felt that a difference existed between me and my peers. My friends and co-workers all seemed to have more of a well-rounded education than I had and I guess it bothered me. I came to the conclusion that I missed out by not getting a broad-based education.

I can't really explain it, but there's a difference in the way you can speak to people, communicate with people, and understand other people when you've got an education. It's a worn-out cliché, but it's true: education makes you a well-rounded person. What's a well-rounded person? I can't tell you! That's the thing.

Anyway, I was maturing quickly and I wanted to broaden my scope. I was newly married, I wanted to buy a house, all that stuff. I knew that I had to do more than just take care of myself, so I started taking some college courses at night.

Taking those courses was not easy, but it was something I felt I had to do. I applied myself, studied, and learned a lot. All of my efforts paid off at the end of each semester. The good grades I got made me proud and helped me to view education in a new light. My wife was very supportive of my efforts too.

If I could do things over, I'd have applied myself throughout my entire career as a student and not just at the end. I'll never know where I could have ended up if I did. Also, I would have tried to participate in and enjoy all of the school experiences, in and out of class. I would have joined some of those school clubs too.

Going to night school was one of the best decisions I ever made, but even still, because I was a night student, I missed out on all of the great college experiences. There's a relatively narrow window of opportunity for those types of experiences. You've got to do it when you get the chance.

Later in life, I found out that it was a mistake for me to have followed certain fields of study simply because I thought that it would make my parents and guidance counselors happy. I should have gone into television production, like I always wanted to. It would have been great to have such a creative career. As it is now, I seek out creative outlets for myself. It would have been great to earn a living by being creative.

The best advice I can give is the same thing that I tell my teenage daughter: When you're a student, you don't see over the horizon. Don't discount the process simply because you can't see your destination yet.

When I was in school, I never saw the need for most of what I was forced to learn. But in my *very* first year at my *very* first job, I saw the importance of the math and science skills that I had been taught. As a student, I wasn't able to see that far ahead, but I later learned the value and the importance of my education.

Don't judge your education based upon what you can see now. Think long term. Trust.

 # Now she knows
(Paula, homemaker, 44)

When I was in high school, I got heavily involved with a guy who went to another high school in a nearby town. All of my time was spent at his school, hanging out with *his* friends and going to *his* dances and proms. It's like I never existed at my own school. It didn't bother me then, but it does now.

Recently, I ran into an old friend from high school. After talking to her for only a few minutes, I realized that she had so many great memories. She was involved in sports, clubs, theater, etc. I never did *any* of those things. She didn't mean to do it, but she made me feel pretty bad by telling me all that. I really regret not being involved in school.

It's not something that I'm happy about, but I was a terrible student. It was never officially diagnosed, but I think that I had ADD, Attention Deficit Disorder. Back in the 1970s, they didn't know as much about it as they do now. That's probably why it wasn't noticed by my teachers.

Back in the eighth and ninth grades, I knew that I had a serious problem focusing and paying attention. Before each class began I'd say, "Okay Paula, today's the day you're going to do it. *Concentrate.*" The bell would ring and I would try to stay in the moment, but it wouldn't work. The next thing I knew, the bell would ring and I would walk out of class and realize that I hadn't learned a thing.

During high school, I began to take courses in cosmetology. I really enjoyed that because ever since I can remember, I've wanted to be a hairstylist. My grandfather owned and operated a hair and beauty salon. My aunt and my mother were hairstylists too.

The way my new course schedule was *supposed* to work was that I'd go to these cosmetology courses in the morning and then go to high school in the afternoon. Well, I didn't do that. Because of the ADD thing, I really hated high school and stopped going altogether.

Eventually the school called my parents and requested that I drop out. This upset my mother because she wanted me to have a diploma. She agreed to sign whatever papers were necessary for me to leave school just as long as I promised to get my equivalency diploma. I took the exam and got my GED. By the way, I passed cosmetology school with flying colors.

I have no real regrets because I don't think that there was anything that I could have done about it. I got a diploma, so that's good.

Out of all of the people I interviewed, Paula was one of the few who said that she had no regrets about being a poor student. I made note of her comments and moved on.

Towards the end of every interview, I ask general questions. The idea behind these questions is to pick up on things that my pointed questions might have missed. Some of the general questions are:

- *If you could go back and change one thing, what would that be?*

- *What do you think is one of the most important things for people to do?*

- *If you could go back and tell yourself something or warn yourself about something, what would you say?*

Paula answered those questions in exactly the same way; she expressed regret over her lack of an education. Because I had remembered her earlier comments about education, I asked her to explain. I didn't press her for an answer, I just kept asking her to clarify her thoughts. We talked about it for a while and she then recognized that she had been contradicting herself. This surprised her quite a bit.

All during this interview, you've asked me about good decisions and bad decisions. When it comes to good decisions, my answers are spread out all over the place; I talk about my kids, my mom, or whatever. When you ask me about bad decisions, my answers keep bringing me back to one thing: dropping out of school. Even now, I tell myself that dropping out was no big deal, but it must be a big deal because otherwise I wouldn't keep thinking about it. All right, I guess it *is* a big deal.

If I could go back and change one thing in my life it would be to stay in school. I would have liked to have gone to college too. I wish that my ADD could have been diagnosed and that I could have found some way around it. I really regret not being more educated.

The importance of education wasn't instilled in me when I was growing up. In *my* home, with *my* kids, my husband and I stress education. I tell my kids to absorb knowledge, whether it's in school or out of school. My kids will not make the mistakes I made. They will understand the importance of education. Education and knowledge make tough roads in life easier. No matter what you do with it, get an education.

Turn the other cheek?
(Sheila, retired elementary school teacher, 60)

I was an average student. My grades were good enough to get me where I wanted to go, so I'm pleased with my academic record. There were a lot of emotional stresses at the time that distracted me from being a really good student. In addition to all of the hormonal changes that everyone experiences at that age, I was a social outcast. Kids teased me.

I threw *big* pity parties for myself. Because of all of that, I tried to minimize my contact with other kids. I didn't participate in any school activities or clubs, which kept me even more isolated. Hiding from my peers helped me to deal with the symptoms of my problems, but not the problems themselves. It wasn't the right thing to do, but I didn't know any better.

When you're a kid with problems and you don't seek out adult advice or help, you'll often come up with some foolish solutions to those problems. That's what I did and it solved nothing. I had *no* adult guidance and the truth is that you can't always solve your problems at that age *without* an adult's help.

I was ashamed to tell my parents what I was going through, although I'm sure they knew. How could they not have? My brother, who was 13 months younger than me, was very popular. That only magnified my situation.

That whole period taught me to have a creative mind. My books became my friends and I lived my life through the heroines of literature. I learned to be comfortable being alone. When everyone was out on Friday nights, what was I going to do, cry? I read my books and daydreamed.

It's not like I got teased every day, but when it did happen, I never stood up for myself. It's important to set limits. You need to let the world know where your boundaries are and what you will and will not put up with. My Christian ethic taught me to turn the other cheek, but if I had set limits early on, I think that I would be in a better place today. To this day, I have a hard time standing up for myself.

I wish that I had fought back against my tormentors. I don't necessarily mean that I should have hit anybody, although I've daydreamed about that too, but there are many possible responses, a whole repertoire of reactions under the umbrella of assertiveness.

Unfortunately, I wasn't encouraged to assert myself when I was young. My mother always said, "Children should be seen and not heard." The school system used to think and act that way too, but not anymore. I was a teacher for years so I know what's available now. The teachers, the school counselors, *someone* is there to listen.

It's okay to be a little defiant as a kid. To tell you the truth, I think it's healthy. If you raise a kid to be a conformist, then when he or she becomes a teenager, they'll have a hard time saying no to bad behavior. When it comes time to decide whether or not they'll drink, smoke, take drugs, commit crimes, or whatever, they'll go along with everyone else.

My grandson is a bit defiant and it bothers my daughter-in-law a lot. I try to tell her that he needs an identity. It wouldn't be right to squeeze the spirit out of him. You can control defiance by offering kids choices. That way, everybody gets what they want and you don't have to crush the life out of the kid.

 Fiefdoms
(Larry, police officer/small business owner, 41)

My area of study in college was motion picture production. I loved it and I was really good at it too. A short film that I directed was very well received at my school's film festival. I probably could have made it my career if I had tried. I regret not giving a shot.

Back then, I didn't have any focus. Not only was I a full-time student, but I was working, commuting, and playing in a band. The biggest distraction was definitely my commute. My round trip drive each day was over two hours. That's way too much unproductive time. Not being on campus made it hard to immerse myself in my studies.

When it came to school or whatever else I was doing back then, I just couldn't stay focused on what I wanted. I should have been thinking of that expression, "Keep your eyes on the prize." It took me a while to develop the mental discipline that you need to focus, but I'm glad I did. It's what's responsible for my success now, both as a police officer and as a small business owner.

I knew a guy in film school who had incredible focus. He wasn't a genius or anything, but he was a machine; he was an animal. He was always working on projects and developing his skills. Three years ago, I saw him on television accepting an Academy Award for special effects. On my son's life, I swear that's true.

Another important thing I learned to do while I was in school was to separate the teacher from the material. In other words, I wasn't so quick to swallow the "party line" on politics, lifestyles, etc. I remember getting angry and confrontational with several teachers because they chose their class, their little fiefdom, as a platform for their political and social views. I signed up for art history, but I was being told how to vote.

Needless to say, my confrontational approach did *not* improve my grades. The bottom line is that I forgot why I was there. I wasn't supposed to be there to defend my views, I was there to get decent grades and graduate with a degree.

This sort of thing is bound to happen in college. One of the smartest things I ever learned to do was just to grit my teeth and hand in my reports on time. I made my opinions heard, but I had to constantly remind myself of where I was and why I was there.

Teachers are extremely cloistered people. Everyone in their world is their subordinate. They live in a world where they get to tell everyone what to do, and they're never wrong. Hey, that sounds like *my* job.

Postscript

Going through flight school and competing for all of those airline jobs fostered in me the notion that an education was essential, and without it you were doomed to drift from one low-paying job to the next. Life has since shown me that that is simply not true. Education is extremely valuable, but it is not essential for success.

Achieving a high level of education can be a valuable thing. However, if you specialize, as I did, you might actually reduce your career and income options. By specializing, you make yourself more vulnerable to any changes that may come. And they always come.

The analogy that I use is this: By specializing, I turned myself into an Allen key. For those of you who might not be familiar with them, an Allen key is a small L-shaped tool. It's a highly specialized and limited use type of tool. It's usually used by cyclists to adjust various parts of their bicycles.

If you need an Allen key for a particular job, you are completely stuck until you get one. There's absolutely nothing else that you can use to get the job done. However, if you don't have any use for an Allen key, it's worthless. Unlike other tools which, in a jam, can be used for purposes for which they were not originally intended, an Allen key can't be used for anything else. It can't open a paint can or a bottle of beer. It can't pound a nail into a block of wood. It can't even turn a screw. Even a paper clip has more versatility.

Like many others, by investing years of my life specializing, I unwittingly walked further and further out on to a narrow plank. I became so specialized that there was really only one thing that I could do: fly big jets. If the one thing that I know how to do goes away, where do I find myself? What happens then?

The devastation of the airline industry in the wake of the September 11 terrorist attacks demonstrated to me that these are legitimate concerns. Not only have the airlines suffered, but many other businesses and industries as well. In a very personal way, it showed me what had already been happening in businesses and industries throughout the United States.

Over the last few years, tens of thousands of people have been told by their employers that they were no longer needed. Tens of thousands of people have been told that their pensions are no longer there. This has happened to working class and professional people in every career field. It is because of this trend that the word *downsizing* has crept into our vocabulary.

Sadly, I'm certain that all of those men and women who were downsized did what they were told back in school:

- Get a good education.
- Specialize.
- Get a good job.

Despite this seemingly good advice, having a good job did not save them. Their specialization did not save them either. One could argue that those two things actually worked against them. When you specialize, you put all of your eggs in one basket. Relying on a "good job" means that you willingly let someone else, namely your boss, watch over your eggs for you.

Specializing and getting a good job are only bad things if that's all that you do. If you do one job and nothing else, if you have no side business, no trap door—in effect, no "plan B"—then you have got no options or alternatives if your job or career goes away.

Recent trends have clearly shown that the only good advice worth taking is the first one listed: get a good education. Regardless of what you want to be or do, that is always good advice. In addition, learn to be versatile. Learn to develop several income streams. Learn to be in business for yourself, even if it's something small. If you're versatile, you'll never end up as an Allen key.

Kindness

*This is my simple religion. There is no need for
temples; no need for complicated philosophy.
Our own brain, our own heart is our temple;
the philosophy is kindness.*

Dalai Lama

Thinking of you

Through these interviews, I have been taught that sometimes, when we extend ourselves to others, we unknowingly change the future. The kindnesses that we show, no matter how small or seemingly insignificant, stay with those who receive them. There is no way to know where these seeds of kindness that we sprinkle will fall, no way to know if and when they will grow to bear fruit, but those who are downstream can tell you some powerful stories about those seeds.

It's strange to think that there could be someone out there right now, someone who you have not even *thought* about in years, who carries with them something kind that you said or did. It's special to them, and when they remember it, they smile.

In many ways, it's very God-like, the power to affect the lives of others. If we understood how much of an effect these small moments have upon others and upon ourselves, what would we do differently? Would we make an effort to sow those seeds every day?

A kid like Bobby
(Catherine, small business owner, 39)

Just this past summer, I went to my high school reunion. Although the actual reunion was held on a Saturday night, the entire weekend,

Friday through Sunday, was made up of parties, picnics, and informal get-togethers. The idea was to maximize our time spent together and to try and include anybody who couldn't make it for the big party on Saturday night.

The first of these get-togethers was set for Friday night. We chose a local bar and let everyone know that this was where their classmates would be gathering. My husband and I arrived at the bar that night and found that the place was packed. We saw that pretty much everyone from my class was there. The next few hours flew by as we laughed and reminisced with old friends.

One of the guys sitting at the bar looked very familiar. I kept catching him looking over, but I thought nothing of it. I figured that if he was a classmate of mine, he would have joined in on the fun. As far as I knew, he was probably just someone that I knew from around town.

The night wore on and people gradually began to leave. Just as my husband and I were getting ready to go, that guy at the bar who looked so familiar got up and walked over to me. Suddenly I realized who he was. He *was* one of my classmates. It was Bobby.

Back in school, Bobby was a really nice kid. I remember him being very fragile though. He was always a bit of a lost soul. He was always so meek that, although I don't remember ever seeing it, I'm sure that he must have gotten picked on by the tough guys in school.

As Bobby walked up to me, I realized that we hadn't seen or spoken to each other in 20 years. We exchanged pleasantries and I introduced him to my husband. Bobby looked great and I told him so. He seemed to appreciate the compliment.

After talking for only a minute or two, I said something like, "So I guess I'll be seeing you for the big reunion tomorrow night, right?" He looked away and shook his head. He said that he had only bad memories from our high school days. He told me that he was still very angry at a lot of people for the way they treated him. He wanted nothing to do with the reunion.

I tried to loosen him up by teasing him a little. I said, "Oh, come on now Bobby. If that's true, then why are you here tonight?" His answer was so sad, but it was also very special too. He said, "I didn't come here to talk to any of those people. I came here tonight hoping to see you. I wanted to talk to you and to thank you." After he said that, he looked away again. I asked him to explain what he meant and why he felt that he had to thank me. He said, "Because you were the only person back in high school who was nice to me."

It's really hard to explain how I felt. My heart broke for him, but I was also very touched that something that I had done had made a difference in his life. I also remember feeling ashamed. I was ashamed of my classmates for hurting or tormenting him so much that he still felt the sting of it 20 years later. I was ashamed of myself for not having realized that this was going on. Why didn't I know about this? Why couldn't I have helped him? Bobby was always such a nice and gentle person; why would anyone want to mistreat him? The whole thing made me feel really guilty.

I tried to hide all of the different emotions that I was feeling. Intentionally, I made the tone of my voice very bright and kept my words positive. I tried to convince him to forget about all of those bad memories and I encouraged him to meet me at the reunion the following night. For a while there, I really thought that I had succeeded. When the big night came, he never showed.

All of this happened about nine months ago. It's the weirdest thing, but I think about it a lot. That story about Bobby and me represents a bit of a paradox. It's good and bad; touching and tragic. I tell that story to everyone I know. I always change Bobby's name to protect his privacy, but I feel like I have to tell that story.

Be kind, for everyone you meet is fighting a great battle.

Philo of Alexandria (25 B.C.–50 A.D.)
Philosopher

Judgment
(Brenda, medical technician, 61)

About 25 years ago, I had a terrible drinking problem. It was just as illegal to drive drunk back then as it is now, but there wasn't all of the attention paid to it like there is today. I'm not proud to say it, but back then I drove drunk almost daily. *Thank God* I never hurt anybody.

One night in particular, I was a little more drunk than usual. I don't remember where I was coming from, but I was trying to get home. I suddenly found myself in an unfamiliar area. I tried to do a three-point turn in a dead end, but I ended up on someone's front lawn. It was dark and I wasn't sure if I had damaged some bushes, a fence, or whatever. All I knew was that I drove into and over something.

The car wasn't stuck. I could have backed up and driven away, but I decided to go up to the front door and confess. A sweet old man answered the door. After I told him what I did, he and his wife came out to see the damage.

As we all walked out to my car, I kept apologizing and promising to pay for the damages. I stumbled on their brick walkway and nearly fell down. I must have looked and sounded like an idiot.

Instead of being upset or angry with me, they were very kind. They could have called the police and had me arrested, but instead, they sort of took pity on me. They said that the damages were small and that just a few dollars should cover it. I wrote them a check right there.

As I was getting ready to leave, the nice old man asked me if I had been drinking. I said yes. He asked me if I was going to be okay to drive home. In a very cavalier way, I said, "Probably not" and turned to go. He said, "Leave your car here. You can get it tomorrow. I'll drive you home." And he did.

When I returned the next day to pick up my car, I saw the *real* damage that I had caused. My car had smashed through some of their bushes *and* through a small wooden fence that lined their driveway. It was obvious that the small check I wrote the night before would *not* cover all of the damages. I wrote them a larger check and left it, along with a note of thanks, at their front door.

My behavior the night before was a hard thing to think about. Being sober and standing in their driveway in the light of day made me feel ashamed. The people who owned that house were kind, decent, and caring people. I was a drunk. Sometimes you don't realize how far down you've sunk until you see someone standing above you. It's easy to forget what it's like to be normal.

As I drove home, I thought about that nice elderly couple and what they had done for me. Maybe they saved my life that night. At the very least, they put me and my needs ahead of their own. It didn't matter to them that I was a drunk, that I had damaged their property, or that I had gotten them out of bed in the middle of the night. They saw me as someone who needed their help. They didn't judge me, they just helped me. I've never forgotten them.

Their treatment of me was one of the things that helped me to quit drinking just a few weeks later. Since that time in my life, I've tried to change. Little things I see in others, good things and qualities that I never had, I now try to emulate. I now believe I'm here for a purpose much bigger than anything I might be doing at the moment.

Every day I look for a sign as to what I might be called to do. Whether it's the chance to help, to be kind, to do something good, or to join charitable organizations, I'm very thankful for the opportunities that have presented themselves. The change in my life has been wonderful. For whatever reason, people who needed help began to seek *me* out.

One day, one of the nice young women in my neighborhood came to my door. She was a tiny little thing, very pretty. She was someone I had been friendly with, but we weren't really friends. She asked if she could speak to me for a moment, so I invited her to come in and sit down.

She seemed pretty calm, but there was something weighing on her mind; I could just tell. She said that she was going to get an abortion. She told me what she was going to do and where she was going to do it. She said that she had no one to help her, no family, no friends, and asked if I could drive her to and from the clinic.

She said that she didn't come over for my advice and she didn't come over for emotional support. Her mind was made up. She just wanted to know if I would help her. Although I said nothing, I wasn't sure if I wanted to get involved.

My thoughts on abortion are the same now as they were then: I think it's horrible. I'm *vehemently* opposed to it. It's one of the worst things I can imagine, but there I was being asked to participate in it. As she talked to me, I thought, *This is a moral dilemma. What am I going to do?*

Strangely enough, the first thing that went through my mind was that elderly couple whose bushes and fence I had destroyed years ago. I remembered that they had put my needs before theirs, that they had not judged me. I remembered how their kindness really affected me.

As corny as it sounds, I felt as if I was being tested. Not by her, but by life. Life was testing me to see if I had learned anything.

I decided that arguing with her after she had made up her mind would have been selfish. It would have been more about what I needed than what she needed. Without ever telling the young woman my feelings about what she was going to do, I said, "Yes, I'll help you."

I drove her to the clinic, I waited for her, and I drove her home. When I say "home," I mean *my* home. I brought her back to *my house*, made her some soup, and let her rest for a while.

Before that day, we had been mild acquaintances, but we moved towards friendship after that. I'm very proud to say that I never judged her. I'm even more proud to say that I helped her.

Charity sees the need, not the cause.

German proverb

The sign of the cross
(Janine, horse trainer, 26)

About five years ago, my uncle passed away. On the day of the funeral, my parents and I rode in the limousine right behind the hearse. It was a beautiful day and I had put the window down so that I could enjoy the weather.

As the funeral procession passed through the streets of Brooklyn, I thought about my uncle and how different our lives were. I grew up in the "lily white" suburbs whereas he lived in the city his entire life. As someone from the suburbs, I always thought that the city was a dangerous and scary place. I figured that the people who lived there were just as dangerous and scary.

The things I saw out the window of the limo backed up those thoughts. Things looked rough. The people looked even rougher. There was graffiti on some buildings and iron bars on the windows of lots of the homes and stores.

There were lots of people on the streets, but nobody looked like me. They were of all different races and cultures. It's not the kind of thing that you ever really think about, but I guess I never saw people like that as being anything like me. I figured that if they lived in such a rough-looking place, then they were all criminals, drug addicts, or whatever.

Another thing I saw was that although I was looking at everyone, no one looked at me. I had always heard that about city people: there's not much eye contact. The whole place seemed so cold and unfriendly.

A few years earlier, there had been some terrible racial violence in the area. It was in all of the New York newspapers and television news. The story eventually got so big that there was some national coverage too. These were the things that were going through my mind as we drove to the cemetery.

Then I saw her. Up the street a bit, on my side of the car, there was a black woman standing at the side of the road. She was young and very pretty, in her mid-twenties, I guess. She had on this really beautiful outfit. Anyway, she was waiting for a break in the traffic so that she could cross the street.

The first thing I noticed about her was that she seemed to be looking at me. As we got closer, I saw that she *was* looking. She was looking me right in the eye. The slow-moving traffic made this eye contact of ours seem to last for a long time.

As our limo passed her, without ever breaking eye contact with me, she made the sign of the cross. Then she reached for a religious medal that she wore around her neck and kissed it. I twisted my head around and looked back at her as we drove away. She stood there on the curb and looked at me for a moment or two, and then she turned and crossed the street.

I sat there sort of frozen. It was like that tough world opened up for just a second. That rough and scary place let its guard down for a moment and let me peek in. And when I peeked in, I saw something . . . beautiful.

It might sound silly, but I was really moved by her simple gesture. She didn't know me, my uncle, or my family, and yet . . . I don't know. I can't really explain it, but I've never forgotten it.

It's embarrassing for me to talk about, but she made me feel really guilty too. See, it's not about that girl making the sign of the cross; it's about what I used to think about certain people. It's about what I never really knew about myself until that day.

I used to see everyone who was different than I was as being *really* different. I figured that if they were *that* different, then they were somehow less than me. But how could someone who was less than me have done something nice like that? And if I really *did* feel that way, then what did that say about *me*?

I try to look at people, and myself, a little differently now. I'd like to think that I would have eventually caught on, but I wonder sometimes about the weird little turn my life took because of that girl in

Brooklyn. It's kind of strange, but she'll never know me or how she helped me to change.

Five years later, and she's still on my mind. Sometimes, some little thing will make me think of her. I can still see her face. If I saw her again, I'd recognize her.

I've gotten in the habit of making the sign of the cross now whenever a funeral precession passes by. I don't really know why. It's just something that I do.

The deeds you do today may be the only sermon some people will hear today.

Saint Francis of Assisi (1182–1226)
Founder of the Franciscan order

Passing by
(Peggy, associate professor, 63)

Back in the 1970s, I was driving home from a college where I was taking night classes. I was going for my Master's in Business Administration. Back then, I lived way out in the middle of nowhere. Quite a bit of time could pass before you'd see another car on the road at night.

As luck would have it, I ran out of gas on a really dark stretch of the parkway. It was pitch black out and the temperature was right around freezing. This was decades before cell phones, too. I didn't know what to do.

I kept thinking that I would freeze to death or that I'd get kidnapped or worse. Should I get out and walk? Should I wait it out?

After a long while, I saw some headlights. As they got closer, a car pulled over and drove up right behind me. I was relieved, but at the same time I was scared to death. Whoever was behind the wheel of that vehicle could be there to help me or hurt me.

A man walked up and tapped on my window. He asked me if I needed any help. I rolled down the car window about a half an inch and asked him to call my husband for me. I even tried to hand him a dime through the crack in the window. Thirty years ago, you could make a call for a dime.

He said, "Oh no. It's too cold out here. Let me give you a lift in my van." I was *terrified*. I thought, "A van! Isn't that how all of those weird guys abduct women?!" I said, "I'm sorry, I can't do that." He tried to reassure me by telling me that his wife and kids were in the van too.

I wasn't sure what to do. It was extremely cold and I figured that I had to choose between freezing to death and taking a chance that this guy was a decent person. I took a chance.

I got out of my car and walked back to his van. Just as he said, his wife and six kids were sitting there smiling at me. What a relief!

That man drove many miles out of his way that night to find an open gas station. As we drove along, his wife told me that this is what her husband does: he helps people. She smiled and rolled her eyes a bit as she talked about how he always stops to help stranded motorists. With a little bit of pride in her voice she said, "He just can't pass them by."

I had to practically beg him to give me his address so that I could pay him for the gas, but he wouldn't. He said that he liked helping people. He certainly helped me. He helped me get gas, drove me back to my car, and made sure I got safely on my way. The kindness that he showed me was the only reason I was able to get home safely that night.

My husband was relieved to finally see me come through the door. He was amazed by my story and was grateful for the help that I received. We both decided that we had to find some way to repay that man.

Just from my conversation in the van with the man's wife, I knew their name and the town they lived in. My husband and I used the local phone book to track him down.

The next day, my husband sent a thank-you note and a check to him. The check was a bit larger than the amount that the man had spent helping me, but the note my husband included said something about treating the kids to dinner.

Because my husband had used his company stationary, a week later, that nice man showed up at my husband's office to return the check. He said that he couldn't accept it. He said to my husband, "I just saw the need to do something good." He was very polite, but firm. Despite my husband's best efforts, he wouldn't let us repay him.

I thought a lot about what happened to me the night I got stranded and I wanted to do the same for someone else. After I started thinking about how I might be able to help someone, I noticed something. It was something that had always been there, but until that moment I guess I never thought I could do anything about it.

I was teaching sixth grade that year. There was a boy in my class who came from a broken home. I've forgotten the details now — it was almost 30 years ago — but I knew his story. Teachers pick up on a lot of things. Teachers talk in the teacher's lounge about the good kids, the bad kids, and the kids with the sad stories. His story was a pretty sad one too.

The thing I noticed about this boy was that he always shuffled his feet. I always saw him do it, but it really had not registered with me. Now that I was really looking, I saw why. His sneakers were so old and worn that the soles were separating from the rest of the sneaker. He was shuffling his feet to keep the sneakers together.

It was then that I decided to try to help him. A new pair of sneakers wouldn't be that hard for me to afford, and I knew he would really appreciate them. I spent the next few days trying to get a feel for the boy's shoe size.

Being a fairly new teacher, I decided to get the principal's blessing first. I didn't want to make waves. A week later, I brought a new pair of sneakers into the principal's office.

It's funny the things you remember. I don't remember that boy's name, but I can still see the principal holding those new sneakers in his hands. I can hear him saying, "These look brand new. He's never going to believe that they're your son's old pair."

That was the idea I came up with. So that the boy wouldn't be embarrassed or humiliated, I'd tell him that the sneakers had belonged to one of my sons and that he had outgrown them. The principal said it wasn't such a great idea to be buying things for the students, but he was sympathetic to the boy's problem. He knew the boy's story too. He handed me back the sneakers and said that since there was no policy against doing that sort of thing, he thought it would be okay.

It seemed to take forever for the lunch period to come that day. When it did, all of the kids began to file out of the room. Before the boy in question got out of sight, I called to him and said that I wanted to ask him something. He shuffled over to the side of my desk and stood there.

Just as I had rehearsed, I showed him the sneakers and told him the made-up story about where they came from. You should have seen the look on his face when I asked him if he wanted them! I felt myself starting to get all choked up and I fought to keep from crying.

He accepted the sneakers with a big "thank you" and a smile. Without taking a step, he put on his new sneakers and dropped the old ones into my wastepaper basket. I turned away and pretended to fiddle with something in one of my desk drawers. I had begun to get teary-eyed and I didn't want him to see. He then ran out of the room to join his classmates for lunch.

Nothing memorable happened for the rest of the year. After he left my class, I lost track of him. We didn't stay in touch or anything; that wasn't the point of what I did. I *had* to help him. I just couldn't pass him by.

There is no duty more obligatory than
the repayment of kindness.

Cicero (106–43 B.C.)
Roman statesman

A man in Manhattan
(Marek, unemployed, 34)

When I was a sophomore at Columbia University, I found myself in an awkward situation. I had come to the U.S. from Poland legally a few years earlier, but my visa had expired and, for a time, I was in the U.S. illegally. I later got my citizenship, but for a while there I was really scared. I was always looking over my shoulder.

Because of this, I began to have money problems. I couldn't get a job, I couldn't get financial aid, and I didn't want to ask my parents for money. They had money troubles of their own. Besides, I wanted to pull my own weight.

The people who worked in the student services office really helped me out. They had leads on all kinds of jobs available to students, on and off campus. I felt safe dealing with them.

They told me about a man from outside the university who had just contacted them. He was looking for a student who was willing to drive him around on the weekends. The only thing required was to have a car. My parents didn't use their car much on the weekends, so they agreed to let me use it. I took the job and was very excited because it would be a cash job and I wouldn't have to worry about my illegal alien status.

A few days later, I met my new boss. He was a very friendly, heavy-set man in his sixties. He lived alone in an expensive building on the Upper East Side. He was very nice and we hit it off right away.

We met every weekend and he had me drive him all over Manhattan. He visited friends and business associates, he went to the doctor's office, he went to visit his sick mother in the hospital, he went shopping, etc. No matter where I took him, we had a good time. He always seemed happy.

There I was, this 19-year-old illegal alien from Poland driving this rich man around Manhattan. None of that is that strange except when you realize that he treated me like an equal. He was a multimillionaire who could have hired a fleet of limousines to take him wherever he wanted, but instead, he hired me. Maybe he believed that by hiring me, he was helping someone out or looking out for someone. Either way, he treated me like a friend, and we *became* friends.

All during our time together, we'd talk. He was really interested in me and my family. He wanted to know about my background and the years I spent growing up in Poland. He took a real interest in my mother too. He always remembered what I said about her and each week, he'd ask me how my mother's job interview went or how she was feeling—something. It was very nice to have someone care.

More than that, he always gave me and my family gifts. They were not regular or unimportant gifts either: they were birthday presents, Mother's Day gifts, etc. When it came to my mother, he was very generous. If it was her birthday or if it was Mother's Day, he'd go out and buy some very expensive cake or something like that, and give it to me so that *I* could give it to her.

About a year after I started driving for him, his mother died. He had no other family, so he took it pretty hard. He seemed lost and a bit heartbroken after that. A little bit of his spirit was gone, I think.

My schedule changed in my senior year and I wasn't as available to him as I had been before. Instead of getting rid of me, he worked around me. He got another student driver to cover the days when I couldn't make it. This man . . . he kept looking out for me.

We drove together for two years. Towards the end, his health began to get worse. I knew about his weight problem, but I think he might have had diabetes too.

One day, I got a call from his office. His secretary said that he had died. She said that my name was on a list of people to contact in case he owed me any money. Can you imagine this? He was gone, but he left instructions so that *I* wouldn't have any worries. He was *still* looking out for me.

He showed me that it was possible for someone to be genuinely nice and generous to a complete stranger. Before then, I was used to expecting support from family members and friends, but total strangers were just that, strangers, and I never expected anything good from them.

That was 12 years ago, but I still think about him. He was the first person I thought of when you asked me about kindness.

I expect to pass through this world but once; any good thing therefore that I can do, or any kindness that I can show to any fellow creature, let me do it now; let me not defer or neglect it, for I shall not pass this way again.

Attributed to Stephen Ettiene De Grellet (1773–1855)
American (French born) traveler and evangelist

Perspective

*Experience is a hard teacher because she
gives the test first, the lesson afterwards.*

Vernon Sanders Law
Professional baseball player

The edge

Many of the people I interviewed told me powerful and moving stories. All but two of them are scattered throughout this book. This chapter is made up of those remaining two. They have been put here under the heading of "Perspective" because, like the flip of a switch, they transformed the lives of those who told them. Something happened. Something in their lives changed, and they were never able to see things quite the same way again.

The idea of perspective, like others we have mentioned, is elusive. Maybe it only comes to us when it's too late. Maybe it's only when we wander too close to the edge that we see how good things really are. If we listen to those who have drifted towards or have been pushed too close to the edge, perhaps we can learn the lessons without risking the fall.

Fate wears a backpack
(Kevin, operations manager, 37)

A little before 9 A.M. on September 11, 2001, I was at my desk on the 80th floor of 2 World Trade Center. It was then that all of us heard a tremendous blast. Within three or four seconds, I saw thousands of sheets of white and yellow paper floating outside my window. I didn't know what to make of it. A second later, black smoke blocked my view.

I ran to the window and saw more paper and debris blowing out of the 90th and 91st floors of 1 World Trade Center. My co-workers and I didn't think that we were in danger, so we sort of stared at the whole thing in disbelief. The mailroom guy even talked about getting his camera.

Our relatively calm mood ended when we heard the sound of screams. About 20 feet behind us, our managing director and other managers began screaming, "Get out! Get out!" *Everyone ran.*

We ran into the hallway that crisscrossed the center of the Tower and searched for the emergency stairway. Of course, we had had our quarterly fire drills, but everyone used those for socializing. We would just meet in the hallways and *not* listen to where we were supposed to go and what we were supposed to do.

I saw people running to a stairwell that I *knew* only descended two floors, but I still ran toward it. I wasn't thinking. My managing director stepped in and yelled at us to use the staircase by the trading floor.

We all entered the staircase that descended down the center of the building, merging with people already evacuating from higher floors. Given the magnitude of what was happening, the evacuation for the next 35 floors was uneventful. Everybody moved at a steady pace. The slower people kept to the right, and the people who needed to take breaks took them on the landings.

I looked around and saw one of the young guys who worked on my floor. He was a body builder with a lot of piercings and tattoos. He always struck me as being a bit of a wild guy, but there he was, carrying another co-worker down the stairs. Some poor guy's prosthetic limb had fallen off and that young guy I knew was carrying him.

We were passing the 46th floor when suddenly, everything came to a halt. Everyone in the stairwell stopped. Panic started to rise.

Just then, there was an announcement over the PA system. The voice said something like, "There's been an incident in Tower 1. The situation has been contained. Tower 2 is secure. You can continue down to the lobby, rest at the 44th floor cafeteria, or go back up to your offices." We all breathed a *huge* sigh of relief.

Trusting in the voice that came over the loudspeaker, I casually made my way down to the 44th floor and looked for an elevator.

When I got there, I saw that there was quite a crowd of people waiting for their turn to take the first one up. I *almost* made it into that first elevator, but it was too crowded. I waited for a little while and before long, it was back. When the doors opened, I was the first person to get in. More people filed in behind me until it was absolutely full.

The last person to get in was a young guy wearing a backpack. The elevator doors kept trying to close, but they kept hitting his backpack and kept opening. This kept happening over and over again. A few of us started to get annoyed.

Just as I was about to tell the guy that he had to wait for the next elevator to come along, the second jet slammed into the 81st floor of our building. The building was *rocked* by the impact and the explosion. Some of the people in the elevator fell down. Sections of the elevator walls caved in on us, and for a second I thought we were dropping 44 floors.

Thankfully the elevator doors were still open, although we could hardly see anything because of the dust and smoke that was pouring down the elevator shaft. I was at the very back of the elevator and I was scared. I screamed, "Come on! Get out! Get out!" It was only a second or two before we cleared the elevator, but it was rough.

Had I gone up on that first elevator, I would have been at my office on the 80th floor, at absolute ground zero. Taking that second elevator isn't what saved me either. It was that guy with the backpack. He kept those doors from closing. He kept us from going up. If we had started going up just a few seconds earlier, we might have been caught between floors, trapped inside the elevator, or asphyxiated by smoke and fumes. Either way, I doubt I'd be talking to you right now.

After we ran out of the elevator, we found the staircase again and started going down. When we reached the fourth floor, we had to go down the stairs single file to allow room for NYC's bravest to go up. We were running out and they were running in. I looked for my brother-in-law Nick, who was a firefighter, but I didn't see him.

When I finally cleared the building, I saw three of my co-workers and we agreed to stick together. We walked across Church Street towards Broadway. Just before Broadway, in the street, we saw what looked like at least four pints of blood and a shoe. Somebody had jumped or fallen to their death *right there.*

As we headed north, we knew what was happening because of all of the radio reports that we heard. Every car in the street, every store we passed, had the news on the radio. We heard those radios blaring wherever we went.

We were right near Chinatown when we heard that our building, 2 World Trade, had collapsed. We turned to look, but there were other buildings blocking our view. I walked right out into a busy inter-section in order to see the towers. I saw 1 World Trade, but as I kept walking, I saw that there was nothing but smoke where my building used to be.

We tried using our cell phones to call our wives, but no dice. The circuits were busy. My friend's aunt owns a printing shop in China-town, so we stopped there to use one of her phones. That's when I finally spoke to my wife. What a relief. We both cried. It was during that phone call that the other tower fell.

I split from my co-workers, vowing to see them again, and headed over to 34th Street to catch a train home. They had just started run-ning again. The train ride that usually took one hour ended up taking three hours, but I didn't care. Every minute took me closer to my wife and sons. That was all I thought about. That was all that mattered.

Finally, I got to my station and I drove home. When I rounded the corner on my street, I saw that my wife was outside with my two boys. As I pulled into my driveway, I was so thankful to be home that I couldn't hold back the tears.

My wife and I hugged like we've never hugged before. After things settled down, I asked my wife if she had heard from my sister. I wanted to know if there was any news about my brother-in-law Nick. She said that his company was sent to the scene and he was last seen running into 2 World Trade Center minutes before it collapsed.

My sister and her boys didn't leave the house for the next ten days. They were hoping to get a phone call telling them their loved one was all right. They waited and waited for the phone to ring, but that call never came.

That was over two years ago. I'm seeing a psychologist now to help deal with a lot of the sadness. It's a hard thing to explain, but sometimes when you live through something like that, you feel a lot of guilt. They call it "survivor's guilt."

I worked in that building for over seven years. I probably spent more time there than I did in my own house. My brother-in-law visited my building maybe twice in his whole life. I think the first time was in the late '90s when he took his boys up to the observation deck to look out over the city. The second time was on September 11, when he ran up those stairs to try to save people's lives. If I'm going to be honest here, that's a big part of the guilt that eats at me.

After someone dies, it's easy to make a sinner seem like a saint, but that's not the case with Nick. He *was* a great person. He *was* the best. He never thought of himself either. As a matter of fact, one of the last things he said to my sister on the phone that morning was, "What building is your brother in?"

Before all of this happened, I wasn't always the easiest person to live with. I was angry more often than I was happy. Whether it was the way I dealt with my kids or my "road rage," I had a temper and everything seemed to bother me.

It's not clear to me how or why I ended up that way. People just fall into those traps, I think. Nobody sets out to be an irritable and cranky person, but that's who I became.

Coming within three or four seconds of death has changed me. I show my appreciation for my wife and children now, whereas I never used to. I never used to make myself available to my kids. Instead of waiting until my boys were asleep or in school before I'd start working on different projects, I'd do those things *instead* of spending time with them.

Now whenever I leave the house, my wife and sons get big hugs and kisses from me. Instead of giving somebody the finger when they cut me off on the parkway, I back off and try to laugh. My eyes are open.

Don't let me kid you, I'm far from perfect. Whenever I start slipping back into the old me, all I have to do is spend some time with my sister and her three boys. That drives it home every time.

I regret that it took something like this to wake me up. Why couldn't I have been nicer to people in the past? Why couldn't I have spent more time with my boys sooner? Anyway, I guess I'm doing it today.

As ridiculous as it sounds, I worry about something happening to me now. Not necessarily because of September 11, but because if something *did* happen to me, I'd probably be remembered as an angry guy. I don't *want* people to remember me as an angry guy. I don't even want to be remembered as an angry guy who turned things around for the last few years of his life. I want enough time to do things right. I want enough time to be remembered as a good guy, just like my brother-in-law Nick.

We are what we think. All that we are arises with our thoughts. With our thoughts, we make the world.

Buddha

On an October afternoon
(Paul, engineer/project manager for construction firm, 42; and Sheri, small business owner, 41; husband and wife)

Sheri: The biggest lesson that life ever taught me was simply to appreciate what I have. I never realized how great things were until my daughter got sick.

She was only three and a half years old when out of the blue, she began complaining that her arm hurt. We took her to the doctor, but her symptoms didn't go away.

Paul: It was a big mystery at first. The doctors didn't know what was wrong with her. Then the fevers started. When we took her back in, they suggested that she get a bone scan. After that, the doctors said, "Okay, she's got a bone infection. Let's treat it." The fevers continued and it wasn't long before they noticed that it wasn't a typical bone infection. Eventually, they did enough tests to determine what was really wrong with her.

Sheri: The worst moment of my life was when I heard the doctor say the word "leukemia." We drove home that day not knowing if my daughter's type of leukemia was treatable. It was too soon to tell. In the space of one afternoon, we went from thinking that my daughter had a minor problem to thinking that we were going to lose her.

We waited for two days for special test results to come in. During those two days, the worry and the pain was so bad that I wished I was dead. You never think that horrible things like this can happen to you. You always think that they happen to other people, but there we were: face to face with the possibility of losing our child. I honestly didn't think I could survive it.

Paul: We went from thinking and worrying about petty nonsense to thinking that our daughter might die. There are no words to describe those types of feelings. Our lives were put in a tailspin. It was hell.

Sheri: Just when I thought I couldn't make it through another minute, I felt a strange feeling come over me. I think it was the touch of God. From that moment on, I felt that I could handle anything that might happen. No matter what those test results said, I knew that we would deal with it.

The next day at the hospital, we learned that there was an 85% success rate treating the type of leukemia my daughter had. When we found out that her form of the disease was treatable, I felt as if a huge weight had been lifted off my chest. I said, "Okay, now we'll fight for a cure." And we did.

Paul: The doctors told us that we were looking at a two-step process. First, we would need to beat it, and then we would keep it in remission. We were told that the whole thing could take nearly three years.

At the time, my daughter wasn't even four years old when she went through all of those frightening tests and procedures. She was scared. She didn't understand what was happening to her. I was a wreck too.

There were some things that really terrified her. Whenever she had to go into one of those MRI-type scanning machines, she panicked. We tried to do it while she slept, but those machines are too noisy; she always woke up. There was one time when I couldn't stand to hear her scream, so I crawled inside after her. I tried to calm her down, but it didn't work. I yelled for the technicians to shut the thing off, but they didn't hear me. I ended up banging and kicking on the sides of that thing until I got their attention.

Sheri: At the hospital, we were considered the lucky ones. We saw so many sick kids; we saw so many heartbroken parents. My husband and I went to so many funerals. Most of our crying was for other people's children.

Paul: We saw other children die at the hospital. We felt terrible when we saw that, but we also felt lucky. We felt lucky that it wasn't *our* little girl. Then when we'd drive home and see other kids, happy healthy kids playing on our street, we'd feel terribly unlucky. We lived somewhere between those two worlds and it was horrible. It was horrible not knowing for sure which world was ours.

Sheri: Everyone has inner strength. Just because a person isn't tough on the outside doesn't mean they can't be tough on the inside. My husband and I are good examples of that. When we first faced this nightmare, I thought that my husband would be the strong one. He was always the head of the household and he always had strength. I was certain that I would crumble. I felt that I would be hanging on to him just to get through the day. As it turned out, I was the strong one. My husband leaned on me to get through it all. My daughter's leukemia made me find the inner strength to get through the tough times.

Paul: She's right.

Sheri: My daughter is completely cancer-free now. As you might imagine, her struggle with cancer changed our whole family. For example, going through that ordeal showed me that I was not in control. Up until her illness, I was always in complete control of my life. Now I see that no one is in control. That's all the more reason to try to be happy and grateful for what you have.

Paul: I thank God for my daughter and for my life. We did the best we could and played the cards that we were dealt. We won. We were lucky.

Sheri: Every day I have an honest appreciation for everything and everybody. I never want to take any of it for granted again. Don't let me kid you, I still yell and scream at my kids every once in a while, but now I appreciate *everything.*

Paul: On my thirty-eighth birthday, I learned that my daughter had beaten leukemia. No gift will ever be more special than that.

Time

*Begin doing what you want to do now. We are
not living in eternity. We have only this moment,
sparkling like a star in our hand . . . and melting
like a snowflake. Let us use it before it is too late.*

Marie Beynon Ray
Author and pioneer of the self-help movement

As you walk by (The unexpected)

My grandmother said something to me on my seventeenth birthday that I still think about today. It was just one of those simple things you hear all the time and usually discard, but for whatever reason, that day was different. She whispered to me, and I was fortunate enough to hear her.

We were just standing in her kitchen talking. My grandmother was drying off one of her pots but before she finished, she put it on the counter and turned towards me. I was still going on about something, but she got my attention by reaching out and touching me on the arm.

She waited a moment and then said, "Jim, I feel just the same as I did when *I* was 17. I know I look like a little old lady, but you only get old on the outside. I feel perfectly young until I look in the mirror, and then I'm shocked at what I see. Try to enjoy yourself because it all goes by so quickly."

My grandmother's comments surprised me. How could she be shocked by her reflection in the mirror? Didn't she know that she was old? Didn't she *feel* old? How could she be so unaware of the passing of time?

Not knowing what else to do, I smiled and we continued on with our previous conversation. Even though she never spoke of it again, I couldn't stop thinking about what she said. It's been over 23 years, and I still can't.

Before that day, I'm not sure what I thought about the onset of old age or the succession of time. I guess I used to think when you got older, you felt older, you thought older thoughts, and you somehow became different. After listening to my grandmother, I knew that those assumptions were wrong. What *she* had said to me was true. Even if I didn't know how or why, I still recognized the truth when I heard it. And because I recognized the truth, it was as if a curtain of secrecy began lifting off of aging and the road ahead of me.

From then on, whenever I saw someone who was older than me, I no longer thought they were somehow different or that their experiences were alien to mine. I knew the only difference between us, if any, was time. Like a sapling and a towering oak tree, both are the same, just at different places along the continuum of time.

While traveling in New England recently, I was reminded of what my grandmother had said all those years ago. On a picture perfect fall afternoon, I stopped in a quaint small town in Vermont and wandered through an old cemetery there. At the northern end, near the trees, I found a tilted moss-covered headstone that marked the grave of a man who lived and died over 240 years ago.

I knelt there in the leaves and read the worn inscription over and over again until I had memorized it. The headstone read:

> *Pause traveler, as you walk by*
> *As you are now, so once was I*
> *As I am now, so you will be*
> *Prepare for this, and follow me*

Like the words my grandmother said to me years earlier, I found nothing especially illuminating or profound in the writing on that headstone. It stated the obvious, and yet it was very powerful. The simple truths expressed by my grandmother and by the inscription on that stone are hard things to explain. They are the kinds of things we can easily point towards over our shoulders, but usually cannot see when we turn to look for them.

If the concepts of time, aging, and mortality are such obvious ones, then why did my grandmother make the effort to say those things to me? Why did that eighteenth-century New Englander insist those words be carved on his headstone?

Maybe it's because when people reach the end of their lives they gain a perspective that they wish they had had earlier. Perhaps my grandmother and that old Vermonter were just saying what they wished *they* had heard when they were younger. Simply put, the mystery that it seems to take most of us a lifetime to solve is this: *time passes*.

Even though we tell ourselves that we understand how time draws out and that we know about the passing of the days, secretly, we think we have forever. We always think we have more time. If we *really* understood the fleeting nature of time, think of how differently we would live our lives. We would embrace our youth, seize each day, and not put things off.

All of my interviews included questions designed to search for similar experiences or realizations regarding time. If something so wonderfully simple said to me by my grandmother could get me to see such an important piece of life differently, then perhaps other stories, other voices could get others to see the same thing.

This chapter points towards one of the biggest paradoxes in life. Time is inevitable, unavoidable, and therefore completely predictable, and yet none of us seem to think that it will ever catch us. Nothing surprises us more than growing old.

The time will come when winter will ask us:
"What were you doing all the summer?"

Bohemian proverb

A jumbo bag of M&M's
(Greg, graphic artist, 40)

When I was growing up, I had a friend named Stan whose mom was *completely* insane. She was this *huge* Polish woman with a weird drag queen look about her. She had the wild clothes, the wild make-up, everything. She looked like a cast member from one of those sketch comedy shows from the seventies. She was a lot older than your average mom, and I think that sort of added to her whole mystique.

Stan's mom did and said the craziest stuff every time I went over to their house. I mean *crazy*. One time, Stan, his mom and I walked to town. We walked because Stan's mom never drove anywhere. Halfway there, Stan very innocently said, "Hey Mom, should we get lunch while we're down there?" Without saying a word, Stan's mom burst into tears, grabbed Stan's arm, smacked him in the face, and then walked back home. It was *that* kind of behavior that caused me to label her as a nut. Whenever she would say something to *me*, I'd just look over at her and nod, but I'd ignore whatever she said.

There was this one day over at their house that I've never forgotten. The three of us—me, Stan, and his mom—were hanging out in their kitchen. Stan and I were in high school, and it was about a week before the winter vacation was about to begin. He and I were complaining that the vacation was still a week off. I said something like, "Man, I wish we could just erase this week and get to that vacation." Out of the corner of my eye, from across the room, I saw Stan's mother's head snap around to face me.

Like I said, ordinarily, I wouldn't care what she had to say, but that one time was different. She gave me this look. This expression came over her face that I had never seen before. It was like, for a moment, the crazy clouds had cleared from her mind. With a look that was very serious and maybe even a little bit sad, she said, "Never wish away time."

218

That was it. A second or two later, the crazy clouds came back again. Her face changed, and there she was—Stan's mom was back. But for a moment there, it was like she was channeling Plato or Spinoza or somebody.

Don't ask me why, but I was really affected by what she said. I think it was the pure shock of it. I mean, if your dog walked up to you and said, "Hey, play the number 352 in tomorrow's lottery," not only would you remember it *till the day you died*, but you'd play that number too.

That thing with Stan's mom was just some throw-away moment I was never even supposed to notice, but I know I'm going to remember it forever. Every time I find myself wishing for something to happen quicker, I think of what she said. Maybe part of the reason she was such a lunatic was because she felt she had wasted her life.

I just turned 40 two days ago. Now that I'm older, I've begun to see my life in the same way I used to treat one of those jumbo bags of M&M's when I was a kid. When I'd first rip one of those bags open, there were so many M&M's, I never thought they'd run out. I ate them by the handful. When I eventually got down to the bottom, I would eat those things one at a time. I'd savor each one. I'd bite them in half and let them dissolve in my mouth—anything to make them last.

Early on, I used to waste my days by the handful. Now I take them one at a time.

While the fates permit, live happily;
life speeds on with hurried step,
and with winged days the wheel
of the headlong year is turned.

Seneca (4 B.C.–65 A.D.)
Roman philosopher, dramatist, and statesman

Sail away
(Frank, retiree, 67)

I got interested in sailing when I was in my late forties. I read every-thing I could on the subject: books, magazines. I took sailing lessons. It was addictive. I loved it. I still do.

As I got more experienced, I tried to take on bigger challenges.

In the spring of 1984, two other guys and I brought a 40-foot Hunter up from Jacksonville, Florida, to Newport, Rhode Island.

We did it in rotating shifts: six hours on, six hours off. It took about five or six days to bring it up.

I was at the helm at sun-up one morning. Because it was right after a big storm, the sea was wild, but the sky was perfectly clear. The sun was *brilliant*. With that bright sun and all of the whitewater, it looked like I was on a sea of diamonds. I came back from that trip just *dying* to get a boat.

Later that same year, my wife and I did a bare-boat charter. We sailed a 30-foot Cape Dory from Groton to Cuttyhunk and then up to Newport and back. My wife never liked boating too much and the idea of that trip was to see if she'd be able to get used to it. She put up with the rain and the tedium pretty well, but she wasn't won over.

I still thought about buying one, a small O'Day or maybe even Catalina, but what was I going to do? My wife wasn't that interested. She wouldn't have minded if I *did* buy one, she told me so, but she wouldn't have wanted to go out much. My sons wanted to do some sailing but they were both in college and I figured if I got a boat I'd *still* be going out by myself. Where's the fun in that?

The dream of getting my own boat never went away because every-body who knew me kept saying, "Frank, get a boat. When are you going to get a boat?" My wife used to say it too. I came close a couple of times but the idea of spending big bucks on something that only *I* would use didn't sit too well with me. It seemed a little selfish. Besides, it's a big step and I didn't want to jump into it. I wanted to make sure I wasn't being unreasonable about the whole thing.

You know, you don't need to own a boat to go sailing. The Jacksonville thing, the Newport trip—I did *those* without owning a boat. I also went out a few times with a friend who had a 39-foot Pearson. Those were good days but there weren't too many of them. It was his boat and I didn't want to impose. Anyway, I should have done more.

The thing is, I always wanted to single-hand a boat—my own sailboat. Nothing crazy, not around the world or anything, but a journey of a few hundred miles would have been great. I just wanted to get a bit more experience first. I needed a little more time.

I had a mild stroke around three years ago. Because of a small seizure and other complications, I wasn't allowed to drive for nearly a year. The medication I've had to take makes me drowsy, so I've got to watch it. If it's late, sometimes my wife drives.

I've still got the time and the money to go sailing. In fact, now I've got *all damn day*, but my health isn't what it used to be. I'm not that sure-footed anymore and it just wouldn't be safe. *I* wouldn't be safe.

I should have done more of it when I had the chance—when I was younger, when I was healthier. I thought I had time. You know, you just don't think that things will ever change.

I wish I had sailed more.

Time is the coin of your life. It is the only coin you have,
and only you can determine how it will be spent.
Be careful lest you let other people spend it for you.

Carl Sandburg (1878–1967)
American poet and biographer

That sex thing
(Gary, maintenance technician for the U.S. Army, 39)

We were 18 years old when my friend Bill and I enlisted in the Army. Despite some big age differences, we got along great with all of the other guys in our unit. We saw ourselves as just kids compared to all of those old-timers. At that age, we *were* the kids on base.

Because we were the new guys, the old guys used to joke around with us a lot. They'd always say things about how young we were and how much we still needed to learn. One of their favorite things was to try and convince us never to get married. They would harp on that one whenever they'd hear us talk about some girls we were dating or whatever. They'd say, "Never get married! Once you get married, you'll never have sex again!" We used to laugh at them for that one.

Twenty-one years later, now Bill and I are the "old guys." We catch ourselves telling the new guys the same crap that we used to hear. Sometimes it's funny, but it's really weird too. When did we get so old?

My dad used to say things like, "You see this hammer? I've had this hammer for 20 years." I used to think, "Damn, that's a long time." Now I look around and see there's stuff *I've* had for 20 years.

When you're not looking, time passes quickly. You're just going along, living your life, and then it just taps you on the shoulder.

By the way, that "sex thing" is true.

Surely, she doesn't mean it
(Annette, librarian, 61)

You know, my mother used to say, "I feel just like I did when I was younger, but now I'm caught in this older, fatter body." I used to think, *Surely, she doesn't mean it. How can she say that?*

Now I feel the same way.

The 80/20 rule (My perfect life)
(Mark, production manager, 38)

When you're just starting out, you always think your life will be perfect. You see yourself with a perfect wife, a wonderful house, great kids; everything is just right. Even if things aren't perfect at the time, you always think they can still *be* perfect later on.

My life had never been anywhere close to perfect, but I always kept plodding along, hoping and waiting for something. I got caught up in the daily routine and the days just began to stack up. Those stacks of days quickly piled up into weeks, months, and years.

My life went on like that until the day my daughter was born. That was both the best and the worst day of my life. The joy I felt and the love I had for her were amazing, but her birth also woke me up to some really unpleasant things. My daughter was born out of wedlock to a woman who couldn't stand me. This woman wanted every cent I had and, in addition, she wanted to keep me away from my own daughter.

The timing of the whole thing couldn't have been worse. Things at work were falling apart, my financial situation was terrible, and my legal bills were astronomical. I lived in a shabby apartment hundreds of miles away from my friends and family. I had almost no social life. My life was awful.

On top of all that, my daughter was born two weeks before my thirtieth birthday. There I was, staring at the big "three zero" and I felt like I hadn't done anything with my life yet. Besides that, I felt like I had completely screwed up the few things I *did* manage to do.

If you had come up to me when I was 18 and said this is the way my life would be at age 30, I would have said you were crazy. Nobody plans to waste time or to waste their lives, but it happens. While I was snoozing, life was passing me by. I figured that if I just kept stumbling along, I'd get the perfect job, meet my wonderful wife, move into my ideal house, and have my great kids. There I was at 30 with a lousy life, wondering where my perfect life was. Could I ever find it now?

I guess I always thought I had all of the time in the world. That's what everybody thinks, isn't it? I made so many bad choices over the years and sometimes no choices at all. I let life happen *to* me instead of being an active participant.

Well, I think a lot differently now. I try to live differently too, but it's difficult. It's one thing to know how to think and how to be, but it's another thing altogether to go out and *do* it. The planning is easier than the execution.

Have you ever heard of the 80/20 rule? It means that 80% of your results come from 20% of your actions. In other words, only a small piece of what you do every day really matters. Those are the things that improve your life; the rest of it just wastes your time. When I first heard that, it made perfect sense to me, but I didn't live it. It was just another good idea that I tucked away somewhere. Ever since the birth of my daughter, I've been trying to act on it.

To me, the 80/20 rule means that you have to strike a balance between "nice to do" things and "must do" things. There are millions of things we would *all* love to do if we had infinite amounts of time, but we don't. You have to learn to separate the pepper from the fly crap.

One of the things I've always wanted to do was to build a wooden boat. That definitely falls under the category of "nice to do" things. If I ever decided to do it, it would be great, but at what real cost? It would take up huge amounts of my time, take years to complete, and what would it really do for me? I'd miss my daughter's school plays, her dance classes, our bike rides together; everything.

There's nothing wrong with the idea of building my own wooden boat, but for me, it would be the wrong choice. It wouldn't be the best use of my time. I'd rather work on building my financial future now so that someday I can *buy* a boat and have the freedom to do other things and to make other choices.

You can always make more money, you can always buy more stuff, but you can't have more time. That's what I try to tell my daughter. Time is the one thing you have that you can't get more of. I wish I could have understood that when I was younger. I didn't even *begin* to see that until I was in my early thirties.

> *An inch of time is an inch of gold, but you can't*
> *buy that inch of time with an inch of gold.*

Chinese proverb

 # The starter's pistol
(Tracy, paralegal, 26)

My whole life, whenever I've looked in the mirror, I've always seen myself as a kid. It didn't matter if I was 16, 19, or 25; I've always seen myself in the exact same way.

Just recently, I realized that I'm *not* a kid anymore. I'm an adult. I'm a woman. It's a very hard feeling to describe. It's almost like I overslept and now I'm looking at the alarm clock in disbelief saying, "It's *what* time?!"

When my best friend got married two years ago, I was shocked to suddenly realize she was a wife. Then she was a *mother*. I thought, "She's not any of those things. She's not old. She's my friend."

It was little strange feelings like those that caused me to try to get my life going, my *own* life going. Believe it or not, I didn't realize that all that time had passed. It sort of snuck up on me.

There are some positives to being blind to the passing of time. Sometimes you *act* old if you think you're getting old. Maybe you can stay young at heart if you ignore the changing calendar. Maybe that's what I was doing.

Now I'm trying to focus on the positives, the good aspects of noticing the passing of time. It's a big motivator. Lately my brain has been screaming, "Get moving! You're 26 years old, you're single, and you're still living with your parents! Get your life started!"

Dost thou love life? Then do not squander time;
for that's the stuff life is made of.

Benjamin Franklin (1706–1790)
American journalist, author, scientist, diplomat, and inventor

The old guy
(Carl, mechanical engineer/project manager for construction firm, 41)

When I started at my job, I was the young guy working with all of the older guys. Most of them were about 20 years older than me. They were all married and had kids that were damn near high school age. All of their desks were crowded with pictures of their wives, kids, houses, and dogs. Those guys seemed *really* old.

The guys I worked with were always there for me. They helped to show me the ropes and to answer any of my "new guy" questions.

The whole thing made sense. I was the young guy, they were the old guys. That's the way it was.

As the years passed, the age gap between us never changed, so I always had this weird sense that I wasn't getting any older. Sometimes I felt that I'd never reach their age. Even if I worked there forever, I could never catch up to them. They were the old guys, and I was the young guy. I would *always* be the young guy at work.

Just last month we hired a new guy at our office. He's working with us part-time while he goes to school to get his engineering degree. I'm not sure, but I think I'm about 20 years older than he is.

He comes in my office from time to time. Sometimes he asks me questions, sometimes he asks for help. He's a great kid so I have no problem giving him a hand.

He came into my office last week and asked me something. I can't remember what it was, but while I was answering his question, I saw him looking at all of the pictures I have on *my* desk. I've got my son's soccer pictures, his baseball pictures, and my daughter's dance class pictures spread out all over. It was then that it hit me: now *I'm* the old guy.

> *The most unexpected thing that*
> *happens to us is old age.*

Leo Tolstoy (1828–1910)
Russian novelist

 ## When they were 64
(Pam, homemaker, 63)

I remember this one evening 32 years ago when my parents came over my house for dinner. They said there was something important they had been meaning to tell me. From the looks on their faces, I knew it wasn't something to be afraid of, but at the same time, I knew it was something serious.

With a smile on his face and in a calm tone of voice, my father said, "Your mother and I have been thinking and we just wanted you to know that if anything ever happened to us, it would be all right. We're both 64 years old and we've had wonderful lives. We've done everything we've ever wanted to do. Don't worry about what might happen. We're very happy."

I smiled and said all of the things that you're supposed to say when someone talks about death or dying. Whether it makes perfect sense or no sense at all, you're supposed to say, "Oh, don't be silly." So that's what I said.

My reaction was pretty normal, I guess. It seemed a bit weird to hear them talk like that, but from my perspective, it also seemed to make some sense too. After all, I was barely 30 and they were over 60. They were old.

That was almost 32 years ago, but I found myself thinking about it recently because I turned 63 this month. I'm almost the exact same age as my parents were when we had that conversation years ago. When I remembered the things they said to me, when I made the connection, I was shocked. I thought, *That can't be. They were pretty old back then. That's not the way I am. I'm young. I'm way too young to talk about dying.*

You know, I would never even *think* those thoughts at this age. I'd feel seriously cheated if I went now.

 # Hi Buddy
(Abe, parks department trail guide, 75)

I went to a wake not too long ago. It was for a guy I knew from the old neighborhood. I hadn't seen him in years.

In our old neighborhood, people used to call me Buddy. Anyway, while I was at that wake, some little old lady came up alongside of me and grabbed me by the arm. She said, "Hi Buddy." I turned and said, "Oh, hello," but I didn't know who the heck she was. It turns out she was one of the young girls I used to know from the neighborhood.

When we were driving home, I said to my wife, "Did you see that little old lady? Can you believe how old she looked?" My wife laughed at me and said, "Who are *you* kidding? What do you think *you* look like, you idiot? Do you think you're running around out there like some 21-year-old kid?" I laughed it off, but the truth is, yeah, I guess I do.

Blocking for me
(Maria, sales associate, 64)

When I started out in the working world, I was 19 years old. I was the cute young girl at the office. All of the guys I used to work for were *old*. When I say "old," I mean they were probably in their thirties and forties.

Regardless of the age difference, we had a lot of laughs and I fit right in. I always gave myself credit for all of the fun we had. Being the youngest, I felt that it was my energy, my youth, that everyone played off of. I could always get the best out of any situation.

In the job that I have now, I'm by far the oldest one there. About a month ago, I was clowning around with the guys in sales. For a split second, for an *instant*, those old thoughts came into my head. I thought, *Maria, this fun stuff happens because you're the youngest one here. Everyone's drawn to your youth.* I really thought that for a moment, but then I realized I was old enough to be their mother . . . and *then* some.

You have to understand, no one tells you you're old. No one sends you a letter. No one calls you at home and says, "Hi. Today's the big day. You're old!" There's no line you cross. There's no switch that gets flipped.

It's a hard thing to explain because you still feel the same way inside. You're still you. That's why you hear people say things like, "Where did all that time go? *Where did it go?*" They don't say that because they're stupid. They say it because it's true. That's the way life is.

Even though I'm getting older, I just don't see myself as old. My 90-year-old mother, *she's* old. She makes me feel young. The fact that she's still around sort of protects me. As long as she's alive, she's the one who's old, not me.

My mom's been blocking for me for a *long* time. If she ever quits the team, I'm in big trouble.

They say life is long
(Curtis, retired Commander in the U.S. Navy, 53)

My Naval deployments took me all over the world. Three of them took me to Christchurch, New Zealand. It's one of the most beautiful places I've ever seen.

My wife used to listen to all of my stories about New Zealand and she was envious. We talked about going there together, but we kept putting it off. It never seemed like the practical thing to do.

Whenever we talked about going, the thought of spending all that money held us back. Well, it wasn't really the money itself, it was just that we didn't want to spend the money *yet*. It seemed like there was always something needed for the house or the kids. We just kept saying, "We'll go someday. Yeah, someday we'll go."

That's what we did in our house: we put things off. The trip to New Zealand was the biggest thing that we put off, but there were a million things like that that came up all the time. Weekend trips, extravagances, frivolous or fun stuff—all of those things were put on hold. We told ourselves that we'd do those things later. You know, some other time.

Finally, after years of putting it off, we bought our tickets and made all of the arrangements to go on our big trip to New Zealand. It was an exciting feeling. We were *finally* doing it. We were even more excited when the tickets and the information package arrived at the house.

My wife had to play in one of her big tennis matches the day the tickets arrived. At the time, my wife was a competitive tennis player. She played on several area teams. Right in the middle of that match, she fell over. Her whole left side shut down.

Everyone thought it was a stroke or a heart attack, so they rushed her to the hospital. It was only after they conducted some tests on her that they realized she had cancer. A scan of her brain showed 14 tumors.

She was diagnosed with renal cell carcinoma. It was classified as stage four, advanced. There is *no* stage five. They gave her a month to live.

We were three weeks away from our big trip to New Zealand, but of course, her diagnosis changed all that. I cancelled our trip and put all of my energy into my wife. She knew what the prognosis was, but she said that she wanted to fight it. She immediately began an aggressive treatment program.

My wife was very strong in mind and body. She promised herself and my daughter that she'd make it at least until our daughter's sixteenth birthday, which was seven months away. And she did it too. Eighteen hours after she saw my daughter blow out the candles on her cake, my wife passed away.

Since then, my kids and I live our lives very differently. We look at our time together as a gift. We don't put our lives on hold anymore. For instance, 10 days before my daughter started her senior year in high school, she said to me, "Dad, I'd like to surf Malibu before I go off to school." I never would have done that before; not in a million years. I would have said, "You have got to be *kidding*." But that time I said, "Let's go."

It cost me about fifteen hundred dollars for the two of us for the weekend, but it was worth it. I didn't mind. If we waited around for "next time," one or both of us might not be around to do it. I just refuse to put things off now. I'd just as soon go out and do something for the kids rather than sit on the money.

My attitude was the same a couple of years later when she wanted to see Australia. I sent her there for three weeks. *That* trip cost me a lot, but it's only money. What good is any of it if you're dead and gone?

If there's one thing I've learned, it's that you're not guaranteed a tomorrow. With that in mind, I've done some things I never would have done before. It felt good to do them, too. You know, life is just too short.

My advice is to live. You shouldn't live foolishly, but you should live.

Many people die with their music still in them,
Why is this so? Too often it is because they are always
getting ready to live. Before they know it, time runs out.

Oliver Wendell Holmes (1809–1894)
American poet and essayist

I remember

All of this—the idea and the purpose of this book, my stories, these interviews—has been about forethought. This book has always been about what's ahead. The interviews dealt with things that took place in the past, but they were chosen in order to better position the reader for the future.

Although I have benefited greatly from this process, having written this book gives me no immunity from occasionally experiencing some of the same mistakes and regrets shared by those I interviewed. For example, I spent nearly two years seeking out, typing up, and packaging these stories. Some of the most touching and portentous ones dealt with the consequences of neglecting the people we love, and yet very often during the process, I neglected *my own family* in order to create this book. There's a Chinese proverb that says, *It is not the knowing that is difficult, but the doing.* Perhaps knowing is a good enough start.

Whenever I feel as if things are getting away from me, when I feel unappreciative or any time I realize that I'm not in the moment—that I'm not taking the time to really see the sky, smell the air, or be grateful for the time spent playing with my son—I call a friend who always seems to have the perfect attitude and the perfect answer for everything. My friend helps those around him to stay in the moment and appreciate the time they've been given by saying the most interesting and wonderful things. It doesn't matter to me that he says the exact same thing to all of his other friends. It doesn't matter that some of the things he says don't quite apply to me. What matters is that what he says is always true.

A few months before I began working on this book, when I was feeling a bit lost, my friend said this to me: "Think about it. Almost everyone who's important to you is still alive. You're living in the best country in the world. You're not hungry or in fear of death, and by most standards, you lead an enviable life. *When you're old and living in a nursing home, you'd give anything just to come back and relive any one of these days that you take for granted.* Remember, you are a prince of this earth."

My friend had impressed me with his views before, but the effect usually faded. Just like the New Year's resolutions that so many of us make, they can be heartfelt at the time, but easily forgotten. But when I heard him say *those* words, it was different. I saw myself in that nursing home—looking back enviously at who, what, and where I am today—and that I *cannot* forget.

Someday our lives, our families, our friends, and all of the smiles and the good times will be distant memories. As frustrating as our daily routines can sometimes be, today is all we have. It's all that anyone has. And when these days are gone, we will miss them terribly.

Knowing that time is ephemeral is not a cause for concern. It's more like a call to action. It's good to realize that there are limits to the things we take for granted. Looking at our time this way helps us to appreciate what we have and to make the best choices we can. And while we live our lives forward, we should do what we can today to keep from looking backwards tomorrow with regret.

Now whenever I want to stay in the moment, whenever I'm afraid of losing my appreciation for things, I think of my son. I think of how he runs over to me and asks me to play. Thinking about his upturned, smiling face helps me to remember.

When I'm at work, I look down on all of those different cities with wonder. I see them bathed in the low afternoon light, and I remember. Their shadows draw out to the east, and I remember.

I remember that mine is a good life. And I am a prince of this earth.

Interview Questions

LIFE EVENTS AND EXPERIENCES

- If you could go back in time and tell/warn/give advice to yourself, what would you say?

- If you could go back and change any one thing, what would that be?

- Is there anything that you feel you missed out on?

- Is there anything that you have regretted putting off? (Have you put something off so long that the window of opportunity has closed?)

- What are some of the things that you've always wanted to do, but never did? (Or haven't done yet?)

- When you were younger, what were some of the things that you wanted to do? (Dreams? Goals?)

- Do you think that you were prepared for ... (a) marriage, (b) your career, (c) parenthood?

- Have you made any big mistakes? If so, what did you learn from them?

- What's the best thing that's ever happened to you?

- Which one of life's lessons has taught you the most?

- Is there anything that has ever happened to you that you viewed as a turning point in your life?

- Do you ever look back on big decisions or choices that you made in life and say, "I'm sure glad I made that choice"?

- If so, what were those decisions/choices?

- What do you think is the most important thing for people to know or do? (For example: to learn about money . . . to be a good parent . . . to marry the right person . . . etc.) *Why?*

- What has made a difference in your life?

- Who has made a difference in your life?

- Do you ever feel that time has snuck up on you? (Everyone who is middle-aged or older has felt this: that strange feeling when you realize that you haven't seen "Fred" in over 20 years . . . The first time the girl at the store calls you sir or ma'am . . . The first time you realize that you're getting older.)

THE ONE WHO GOT AWAY

- Do you have a story about the one who got away? Someone with whom you might have had a romantic relationship, but because of something you did (or failed to do) it just didn't happen.

- Regrets? (Would you do things differently?)

MARRIAGE

- What's the best thing about marriage? What's the worst thing?
- Regrets? (Would you do things differently?)
- With regard to marriage, what advice, if any, would you give?

CAREERS

- Did you choose a good career for yourself?
- Regrets? (Would you do things differently?)
- Good decisions? (What are you glad that you did?)
- Regarding careers, what advice, if any, would you give?

HIGH SCHOOL

- Were you a good student?
- Are you pleased with your academic record?
- If not, what would you have done differently?
- Were you involved in sports/theater/clubs?
- Did you have an active social life?
- Regrets? (Would you do things differently?)
- Good decisions? (What did you do that you're glad you did?)
- Regarding high school, what advice, if any, would you give?

COLLEGE

- (Same as above)

MONEY

- Are you good with money? How has that knowledge or lack of knowledge affected you?

- Regrets? (Would you do things differently?)

- Good decisions? (What did you do that you're glad you did?)

- Regarding money and finances, what advice, if any, would you give?

GRUDGES

- Did you ever hold a serious grudge against anyone? How did that turn out?

- Regrets? (Would you do things differently?)

PARENTS

- Did you have a good relationship with your parents? What made it good or bad?

- What positive *and* negative examples did they set for you? (For example, "My parents were supportive, so I'm supportive of my kids." "My parents hit me and I hated it, so I *don't* hit my kids.")

- Regrets? (Would you do things differently?)

CHILDREN

(Same as above)

SIBLINGS

(Same as above)

GRANDPARENTS

(Same as above)

FRIENDS

- Do you have good friends? (If yes, what makes them good? If not, why not?)

- As far as your friendships are concerned, do you have any regrets? (Let any good friends down? Let any slip away?)

- With regard to the subject of friendship, what advice, if any, would you give?

KINDNESS

- Was there ever a time when anyone showed you an act of real kindness? Perhaps a stranger?

- Have you ever shown anyone an act of real kindness?

- In either example, what did it mean to you?

RETIREMENT

- What's been the best thing about it? What's been the worst thing about it?

- What about retirement has been unexpected or unforeseen?

- Who else should I be interviewing?

Index

A note for my mother 106

Abe, parks department trail guide 228

abortion 190

Abriti, advertising agency owner 20

abuse 139

Academy Award 178

achievement 95

ADD 174

addiction, addictive 100

adventure 27, 38

advice 1, 98, 136, 160, 171, 173, 181, 190, 232

affair, affairs 125, 136

affect (someone's life) 101

affirmations 78

afraid (*also see* "fears") 37, 73

Africa 35

Agathon 100

Air Force 86

Air National Guard 168

alcoholic, alcoholism 114

Alicia, management consultant 162

Allen key 179

Alps, The 140

Amiel, Henri-Frédéric 76

Amy, flight attendant 45

An American in Florence 25

Andy, mechanic 113

Angela, receptionist 116

anger 28, 108

Annette, librarian 222

Anthony, department store manager 109

Anthony, retired NYC police officer 30

appearance 61

appreciation 209, 211

approval 102

Aristotle 132

Arlene, retired elementary school teacher 32

Army 22, 33, 222

ashamed 97, 115, 189

assertiveness 85, 177

As you walk by (The unexpected) 215

attic 116

attitude 29, 232

attorney 87

Australia 231

backpack 205

Baking in a boxcar 21

bald 56

Barefoot in Toronto 137

Barry, retired counselor 18

belief 78

Bet your bottom dollar 150

Billings, Josh 105

Block Island 9

Blocking for me 229

Body of evidence, A 10

Bohemian proverb 217

Bombay 20

bombing, bomb 34, 86

Bonaparte, Napoleon 17

Borrowed man, A 125

Boston 53, 150

bottom dollar 151

Broadway 206

Brenda, medical technician 188

Bronx, The 30

Brunelleschi 25

Bryan, William Jennings 55

Buddha 101, 208

Bujold, Lois McMaster 115

Bulgarian proverb 56

burns 58

California 87, 149, 164

Canada 7, 66, 148

cancer 97, 102, 211, 231

Cannes 140

career, careers 63, 70, 79, 83, 87

Carl, mechanical engineer/ project manager for construction firm 226

Carol, professor of accounting 166

Carry that weight 113

Cash or charge? 149

Catherine, small business owner 185

challenge 170

chance 32, 79

change, changes 27, 30, 89, 131

Chantal, sales rep 137, 148

charming 56

cheater 137

Chicago 47

Chinatown 206

Chinese proverb XIII, 13, 111,
146, 162, 225, 232

Chinks in the armor 120

choices xv, 24, 68, 89, 90

Chris, engineer/project
developer 81

Chris, small business owner
100, 143

Christmas card 112, 114

Christmas Carol, A 3

Christmas morning 30

Cicero 196

Cindy, corporate manager 125

Citizen Kane 41

Claire, customer service agent
111

close-minded 30

cocaine 100, 144

coin 221

Cold War, The 34

Coliseum, The 152

college 20, 23, 28, 44, 66, 68, 76,
96, 102, 106, 143, 145, 148, 150,
157, 162, 166, 168, 170, 171, 176,
178

Columbia University 166, 197

comfort, comfortable 79

commitment 128

complacency 77

computer 11, 20, 69, 74, 129

confidence 15, 78

connections 107

consequences 232

conversation 76, 77, 126

Courage 112

CPA 167

Craig, airline pilot 11

Crazy money 148

credit card 145, 150

creative 20

Curtis, retired Commander in
the U.S. Navy 230

Cute and funny 170

Cuttyhunk 220

Cyber sex and the Sirens' song
129

cynicism 88

Da Vinci, Leonardo 25

Dale, airline pilot 121

Dalai Lama 183

damnation 115

Dan, computer engineer 171

Danny, project supervisor 21

Darlene, wedding planner 68

Darren, attorney 83

date, dating 45, 138

dealing with people 82

death, dying 97, 103, 109, 113, 114,
116, 119, 216, 227, 231

Debbie, educational administrator 170

debt 145, 150

decisions 32, 131

Decisive moments 28

Degree, degrees 18, 24, 27, 29, 68, 73, 77, 148, 149, 150, 160, 167, 168, 169, 179, 226

De Grellet, Stephen Ettiene 199

Dennis, massage therapist 135

desires 132

desperation 91

determination 12, 86

diabetes 198

Did Pete call? 52

discipline 178

divorce 48, 89, 99, 134, 135

doing 232

Donna, retired court stenographer 114

Dorothy, professional musician 106

Doug, entrepreneur/former airline pilot 25, 87

dreams 10, 20, 32, 70, 167

Dreams and awakenings 5

drifting 22

drugs 144, 164 (drug abuse 160, drug addicts 113, 191)

drunk, drinking 21, 24, 26, 100, 109, 114, 188

Dryden, John 153

Ebner-Eschenbach, Marie von 157

echo effect 86

education 19, 20, 22, 82, 98, 106, 160, 168, 171, 175, 179

effect (on other people) 99, 101

elevator 88, 205

Eliot, George 91

Eliot, T. S. 39

embarrassment 73, 97, 115

Emerson, Ralph Waldo 118

Emotional ice cube 102

emotional quotient 85

enemies 132

enthusiasm 20

Europe 25

Eve, mother/homemaker/small business owner 132

Experience, experiences 1, 9, 19, 67, 152, 162, 167, 170, 173, 201, 216, 221

excuse 48

Eyes open 74

FAA 86

failure 73

family 93, 95, 99, 107, 111, 112, 115

fantasy, fantasize 50

Fate wears a backpack 203

FBI 86

Fear, fears 8, 32, 35, 85, 100, 160

ferry boat 41

Fiefdoms 178

fight 111

finances, financial 143, 147

finger 26

fire 58

firefighter 206

fishing 121

flight school 66, 179

Florence 25, 86, 89

Florida 66, 220

focus 16, 148, 160, 178, 226

For my grandmother 118

Forest Hills 55

forgive, forgiveness 96, 104,
    108, 114, 120

France 140, 149

Frank, retiree 220

Franklin, Benjamin 226

Friend to a friend 117

friends, friendship 18, 61, 93,
    96, 100, 118

fulfilled 71

funeral 191, 210 (*also see* "wake")

Galilei, Galileo XVII, 25

game playing 47

Gandhi, Mahatma 16

Gary, maintenance technician
    for the U.S. Army 222

German proverb 190

Germany, East Germany 34

Gibran, Kahlil 108

gliders 65

Gloria, advertising executive 96

glory 17

goals, goal-setting 78, 145

Goethe, Johan Wolfgang von 70

Going to the chapel 68

Gone fishing 121

Good girl, bad girl 45

gorilla 36

Grand Canyon 152

grandfather 102, 108, 119

grandmother 119, 215

Greg, graphic artist 218

grindstone 105

Groton 220

grudges 108, 113

guidance counselors 19, 166, 173,
    177

guilt 115

guitar 100

Guitars and amps and crap 143

habits 11

hammer 222

Hamptons 129

haunt 42, 96

Hawaii 133

health 11, 153, 221

heart attack 65

heartbreak, heartbroken 127

Helen, homemaker 117

Her life 116

Herbert, George 114

Hi Buddy 228

high school 157

Holmes, Oliver Wendell 89, 232

homesick 33

Hoping he'd turn around 55

Horace 45

How cavalier 100

Hugh, government employee 98

humility 29

Hyannis 9

I *am* smart 168

I can't remember 114

I never saw him again 108

I remember 232

I wouldn't presume 125

identity 79

If you're going to San Francisco 18

ignorance 47

illegal alien 197

immaturity 99, 118

immunity 232

In a whisper 1

independence 8, 73, 85, 139

India 20

inexperience 151

influence 166

innovator, innovative 20, 21

instincts 148

Internet 69, 101, 129, 140

Interview questions 235

Iron men 104

irresponsibility 150

Italy 149

Jacksonville 220

Janine, horse trainer 191

Jeff, network administrator for the Air National Guard 168

Jeff, computer technician 74

JFK Airport 35

John, attorney 149

Judge, judgment 128, 155, 173, 188, 190

Julliard School of Fine Arts 17

Jumbo bag of M&M's, A 218

Keller, Helen 38

Kelly, licensed practical nurse 107

Kenya 35

Kevin, operations manager 203

Kid like Bobby, A 185

Kilimanjaro 36

kind, kindness 183, 185

Know money, or no money 146

knowing 232

Larry, police officer/small business owner 82, 178

Laura, mental health counselor 118

Law, Vernon Sanders 201

lessons 1, 23, 65

leukemia 209

lie 97

life-changing event 60

life passing by 223

Lisa, dental assistant 108

Lisbon 25

loan 148, 150

Long Island 96, 106

love 123, 125

Love is a girl's best friend 132

Looking back: Whispers of high school, college, and the armed services 157

Lori, retired elementary school teacher 13

Lou, retiree 10

lunatic 219

Lynne, freelance photographer 52

M&M's 219

Magic hour 107

magnets 109

Making her own way 32

Malibu 231

Man in Manhattan, A 197

Manhattan 106, 197

manipulate, manipulative 119

Marek, unemployed 197

Maria, sales associate 229

Mark, production manager 223

marry, marriage 46

Martha's Vineyard 9

Mary, retired elementary school teacher 79

Masi warriors 37

Matthew, stockbroker 150

Mensa 84

Michelangelo 25

millionaire 146

mirror 225

Mistake, mistakes 29, 33, 44, 56, 83, 86, 98, 99, 104, 106, 110, 118, 121, 125, 149, 150, 160, 169, 173, 176

misunderstandings 126

Molière 62

money 143

Money and finance 141

mourning 27

mountain, mountains 27, 36, 140

Mumbai 20

My mentor 111

My money 143

naive 23, 82, 84, 150

Nantucket and a fleeting glimpse 7

Native American proverb (Dakota tribe) 93

Navy, Naval 230

neighborhood 30, 228

New England 7, 66, 216

New Hampshire 52

New York City 17, 21, 106, 128

New Zealand 230

Newport 9, 220

Ngorongoro crater 36

Nick, physical therapist 112

Nine years and eleven months 76

Nirvana 108

No Andy Warhol 20

Nobody gets into Stanford 162

Now she knows 173

nursing home 233

Ohio 135

old, older 226, 228, 229

On an October afternoon 209

Our friends and family 93

Out of pocket 144

overcome 32

overweight (*also see* "weight") 10, 13

Pam, homemaker 227

parents 20

Passing by 193, 223

passionate 80

path 2, 27

Paul, engineer/project manager for construction firm; and Sheri, mother/homemaker/ small business owner; husband and wife 209

Paula, homemaker 173

Peggy, associate professor 193

People knowledge 83

people skills 81

perfume 98

perspective 29, 201, 203, 217

Phelps, William Lyon 63

Phil, accountant 43

Philippines, The 33

Philo of Alexandria 187

plan 147

Plato 219

Plutarch 98

Poland, 197

Polish 218

Political science 81

ponytail 55

Porsche 159

portentous 232

Portugal 25

post-traumatic stress disorder 87

Postscript 179

Preface xv

pride 113

priorities 71

prince of this earth 233

proactive 54

problems 176

procrastination 42

promise 122

Purely by accident 159

put off 153, 230

racial, racism 30, 191

Raffaello 25

Ramifications 98

Rana, pharmaceutical research chemist 164

rationalization 126

rats 37

Ray, Marie Beynon 213

Ray, medical professional 57

rebound 135

reflections, James Green xv, 1, 7, 35, 41, 65, 86, 90, 95, 120, 125, 143, 153, 159, 179, 185, 203, 215, 232

Reggie, sanitation worker 146

regrets 2, 9, 42, 56, 73, 114, 120, 143, 161, 171

rejection 135

relationship 45, 95, 125

Relationships, love, and marriage 123

responsibility 74, 121

reunion 185

Rhode Island 9, 220

Rick, partner and branch manager of a brokerage house 76

risk 12

Risk and reward 11

Roberta, marketing assistant 72

romance, romantic 57

Rome 143, 152

Roman ruins 25

Ron, technician 47

Roosevelt, Eleanor 25

rose garden 39

rusty 155

Rwanda 36

safari 35

Sail away 220

sailboat 221

Saint Francis of Assisi 193

Saint John's University 55

Samantha, educational administrator 152

Sand, George 134

Sandburg, Carl 221

Santa Barbara 164

sarcasm 88

Schiller, Johan Friedrich von 167

Scrooge, Ebenezer 3

seeds 185

self-centered 118

self-confidence 135

self-defeating 44

self-discipline 169

self-esteem 127

self-image 13

selfish 220

self-loathing 15

self-regard 85

self-worth 114

Seneca 219

September 11th 12, 27, 86, 180, 203, 207, 208

Serengeti 36

sex 45, 61, 129, 139, 170, 222

shadows 85, 234

Shakespeare, William 47

Sharon, cashier 16

She liked me 135

Sheila, retired elementary school teacher 176

Sheri, administrative assistant 55

Sinners and saints 96

Sitting on my hands 47

smell the roses 18

sneakers 195

snowflake 213

Sophocles 11, 129

Spain 25, 163

Spanish 163

specialize 180

Spinoza 219

Spokane 130

Staël, Germaine de 104

Stanford 162

star 111, 213

starting one's own business 69, 73

starting over 73

Steve, architect 129

stockbrokers 77

Stowe, Harriet Beecher 116

Stress, stressful 17, 65

Strong son, A 109

struggle 29

success, successful 69

Succinctly speaking 21

supermarket 149, 150

Surely, she doesn't mean it 222

surf 231

Suzy, educator/former corporate executive 70

Swift, Jonathan 156

Tanzania 35

target 76

Ted, financial planner 104

telescopes 25

Ten feet tall and bulletproof 65

tennis 230

terrorists 86, 180

That sex thing 222

The dancer 16

The echo effect 86

The edge 203

The 80/20 rule (My perfect life) 223

The faceless man 49

The gift 87

The natural choice 79

The old guy 226

The one who got away 39

The only thing 95

The pretty lady 13

There's something about Stephanie 57

The richest man in the graveyard 153

The role of the airhead 164

The river visual 90

The sign of the cross 191

The starter's pistol 225

They say life is long 230

Thinking of you 185

Thoreau, Henry David 10, 91

Three letters 166

time 213

timidity 42

Tim, law enforcement officer 28

Today 152

Todd, customer service agent 144

Tolstoy, Leo 227

tomatoes 80

Toronto 138

tracks 93

Tracy, paralegal 225

transfer 83

transition 28

travel 32, 152

trust 128, 171

truth 216

turning point 14

Turkish proverb 120

Turn the other cheek? 176

TWA 67

Twain, Mark 5, 79, 122

ugly 13

unappreciative 232

underachiever 159

Underlined in black 43

unhappiness 102

Unknown, Author 51

unstable 128

unworthiness 14, 163

values 71, 106

Vancouver 131

Van Gogh, Vincent 35

Vermont 216

versatility 181

Vicki, real estate agent 49

Victorian-era 15

victory 132

Vietnam 144,

Vietnam War 33

Virgil 74

Virunga Mountains 36

vision 27, 41

Vivian, corporate manager 102

wake 228

Washington D.C. 90

Washington National Airport 90

Washington State 130

Wearing a white dress 41

weight problem 13, 111, 198

well-rounded 172

When they were 64 227

Whisper and the Dark continent, A 35

whispers 2, 38, 96, 157, 215

Who I am 70

Wilde, Oscar 141

Will, retired small business owner 21

withdraw, 145, 170

Windows that open and close 82

World Trade Center 203

worthy 139, 163

Your own totem pole 72

youth 8

Zen saying 85

To order additional copies of
If There's One Thing I've Learned . . .
check your leading bookstore or use this form.

ON-LINE ORDERS:	*For fastest service, order online:* www.SoundViewPublishing.com
TELEPHONE ORDERS:	Call 1-888-529-3496 toll-free. *Please have your credit card ready. If you cannot get through, please try again.*
FAX ORDERS:	Fax this form to 1-631-899-2487.
POSTAL ORDERS:	Sound View Publishing, Inc. P.O. Box 696 Shoreham, NY 11786-0696

Please send me _____ copies @ $ 19.95 each $ _____

Postage and handling (within the U.S., add $4 for
    the first book and $2 for each additional book) $ _____

New York residents, add $1.75 sales tax per book $ _____

Total $ _____

❑ Enclosed is my check or money order in U.S. dollars (payable
to Sound View Publishing)

Please charge my:

    ❑ Visa   ❑ MasterCard   ❑ American Express   ❑ Discover

Card # _____

Name on card _____

Exp. date _____

please print:

    Name _____

    Address_____

    City_____

    State _____ Zip _____

    Phone (   ) _____

    E-mail_____

Please allow 2 to 3 weeks for delivery.